Library Technology and User Services

CHANDOS
INFORMATION PROFESSIONAL SERIES

Series Editor: Ruth Rikowski
(e-mail: Rikowskigr@aol.com)

Chandos' new series of books is aimed at the busy information professional. They have been specially commissioned to provide the reader with an authoritative view of current thinking. They are designed to provide easy-to-read and (most importantly) practical coverage of topics that are of interest to librarians and other information professionals. If you would like a full listing of current and forthcoming titles, please visit www.chandospublishing.com or email wp@woodheadpublishing.com or telephone +44(0) 1223 499140.

New authors: we are always pleased to receive ideas for new titles; if you would like to write a book for Chandos, please contact Dr Glyn Jones on email gjones@chandospublishing.com or telephone number +44(0) 1993 848726.

Bulk orders: some organizations buy a number of copies of our books. If you are interested in doing this, we would be pleased to discuss a discount. Please contact on email wp@woodheadpublishing.com or telephone +44(0) 1223 499140.

Library Technology and User Services

Planning, integration, and usability engineering

ANTHONY S. CHOW AND
TIMOTHY BUCKNALL

CP
CHANDOS
PUBLISHING

Oxford Cambridge New Delhi

Chandos Publishing
Hexagon House
Avenue 4
Station Lane
Witney
Oxford OX28 4BN
UK
Tel: +44 (0) 1993 848726
E-mail: info@chandospublishing.com
www.chandospublishing.com

Chandos Publishing is an imprint of Woodhead Publishing Limited

Woodhead Publishing Limited
80 High Street
Sawston
Cambridge CB22 3HJ
UK
Tel: +44 (0) 1223 499140
Fax: +44 (0) 1223 832819
www.woodheadpublishing.com

First published 2012

ISBN: 978-1-84334-638-8 (print)
ISBN: 978-1-78063-290-2 (online)

© Anthony S. Chow and Timothy Bucknall 2012

British Library Cataloguing-in-Publication Data
A catalogue record for this book is available from the British Library.

Typeset by RefineCatch Limited, Bungay, Suffolk
Printed in the UK and USA.

To Theresa, Alex, Maegan, and Emma – your love, support, and influence help make all things possible; every day you remind me of how blessed I really am.

To Nancy, Kevin, Carolyn, and Michael – for putting up with me.

Contents

Contents

List of figures and tables

Figures

Tables

Acknowledgements

Dennis Frye and Tommy Joseph for sharing with us their technology infrastructures and immense knowledge and expertise.

Theresa, Alex, Maegan and Emma for giving us the time and support to write this book.

Amy Figley for her outstanding copy-editing and research.

All our students, friends and colleagues who contributed their knowledge, expertise, ideas and feedback throughout this process.

Foreword

Whether you are a practicing librarian or a Library and Information Studies student preparing to launch your career, *Library Technology and User Services* is right on time with what you need to know in order to leverage technology to provide users with greater access to resources in a more efficient and effective manner than ever before. There are many of us who may know we need to bring new or better technologies into the library, but have no idea where to begin. There are others willing to jump in with both feet and embrace the latest technology fads, often at the expense of the library budget. Chow and Bucknall do an outstanding job by offering a careful, step-by-step approach for systematic planning, budgeting and leveraging technology to best meet the information needs of users. Along the way, they introduce you to the current technology trends while explaining the necessary terminology, without losing the reader in techno-jargon. After reading this book, I now feel poised to act as a catalyst in my library for taking the steps to better match technologies with the needs of my users!

Rebecca Croxton, MLIS, Johnson & Wales University
Library, Charlotte, NC

Chow and Bucknall's comprehensive look at how information technologies are being used for both access and library service reminds us how at once the library is a place of not only storage for collections of books but how that place can best be the one that intricately and purposely serves our every information need: whether that need is access to information, learning to use information, or connecting with others. As a Director of Instructional Technology and Media for a K12 school system, I am often asked the question of how the library remains viable in a sea of students with iPods. Chow and Bucknall help us all gain a renewed perspective and appreciation for the compelling requirements of modern librarianship and how, now more than ever, it can be applied to exceed our every information need.

Dennis Frye, Director of Instructional Technology and Media,
Rockingham County Schools

Today's digital technologies are of an order and form to truly transform man's continuing quest for enhanced learning and understanding. More than ever, our modern academic libraries are challenged to embrace these technologies and apply them in ways that optimize their potential for developing and supporting services of the very highest quality. Upon examination, what we find is that today's libraries are confronting and meeting that challenge in the most salubrious ways, creating and implementing new technology-based services that are imaginatively advancing our primal human yearning to discover and to know.

Dana Sally, Dean of University Libraries at
Western Carolina University

This book is geared to the upper level master's degree candidate, the practitioner and of course anyone that is curious about how librarians provide and plan for access to technology. The authors wrestle with the theories of 20th century library management practices in a 21st century library environment. How do we change our management perspectives to relate to this new technology rich environment and provide high quality and affordable services in the digital age? Looking at needs assessment instead of outcomes, understanding technology and how it impacts our patrons and not just offering our patrons access to technology is the challenge of this new paradigm. The authors recognize that librarians have often been at the forefront of offering patrons the kind of technology that they need to complete research, to locate books and other information sources and to have access to the important software and digital content that makes life in the 21st century possible. They also realize that librarians are not the best at planning how to implement, budget and subsequently manage that technology. With primers on infrastructure backbone and how it works, access to the Internet and how it is managed and sections on how to make sense of budgeting when obsolescence is certain, this book provides answers and very workable models on how to manage and succeed at this very difficult concept of technology at the crossroad of information access.

David Bryden, Director of High Point University Libraries,
High Point, NC

It is both refreshing and thought provoking to find a book that so effectively puts into perspective the integration of technology into the historical role of a library. The insights brought to bear on this important topic are shared by authors Tim Bucknell and Dr. Anthony Chow, who have focused their careers on searching for the most efficient and effective manner of disseminating information to an ever diverse and increasingly media savvy population. They recognize that technology must be the means of distributing this information, yet introducing and integrating this dynamic resource into libraries is a challenge. Their book develops this theme by tracking library trends in academic, public and school libraries and effectively designing methods to identify and meet the needs of these user groups. Through careful planning, setting constructive goals, implementing robust technology and thoughtfully evaluating the end results, they ensure a successful outcome. With *Library Technology and User Services*, they have created a valuable work that will serve as a blueprint for students, faculty and practitioners who seek to understand how technology can effectively expand and enhance user services and resources in a library environment. Despite the fact that there undoubtedly will be many technological advances in the future, the means and methods outlined in this book will remain valid and timely in the years to come.

Kathelene McCarty Smith, MLIS, Artifacts, Textiles and Digital Projects Archivist, The University of North Carolina at Greensboro

About the authors

Dr. Anthony Chow teaches library management and technology as an assistant professor in the Department of Library and Information Studies at The University of North Carolina at Greensboro. He has been teaching at the graduate university level for over 11 years and is the author of over 60 academic presentations, articles and books. He has a doctorate in instructional systems (systems design) and master's degree in educational psychology (learning and cognition) and has served as a usability lab director, head of user services and coordinator of online learning. Dr. Chow also serves as an educational consultant specializing in online information and evaluation systems and has overseen the IT for a large academic unit, managed training and quality assurance for an Internet company and oversaw computer based instruction training for a government agency. His dissertation was published as a book entitled *Systems Thinking and 21st Century Education*. Dr. Chow's professional and academic experience has allowed him views of the complex interactions between users and technology from a diverse set of perspectives and settings – as user, as trainer, as IT support, as IT director, usability engineer, as designer and instructor and as a researcher.

Tim Bucknall is Assistant Dean of Libraries and Head of Electronic Resources and Information Technologies for the University Libraries at the University of North Carolina at Greensboro. He holds both an MA (Art History) and an MLS from The University of North Carolina at Chapel Hill. Tim is responsible for many significant library innovations, including the first OpenURL link resolver to go into production and the first large virtual library consortium. He was recently named by *Library*

Journal as one the United States' leading 'Movers and Shakers' within librarianship and has published and spoken extensively on library information technology, IT management and effective evaluation of electronic resources and services within libraries.

The authors may be contacted at:
E-mail: aschow@uncg.edu, bucknall@uncg.edu

Introduction

Today's users expect their libraries to effectively utilize current technologies to enhance the library experience. For people who own computers, technology brings e-books, databases, online articles, the library catalog and other resources and services directly into the home. For those without computers, libraries offer egalitarian access to the wealth of resources available on the information highway. Many libraries also offer wireless connectivity, social networking, electronic books for e-readers, digital reference, Internet and software training classes and much, much more. Technology infuses every aspect of libraries and librarianship and is a key driver of user satisfaction. But given the wide array of library technology options and the widely disparate information technology needs and skills of library users, identifying and providing the most appropriate and cost-effective library technologies can be a significant challenge.

This book addresses that challenge by providing a systematic process for planning, budgeting and integrating technology in libraries. It is written for practitioners, faculty and students. It includes a review of the contemporary research on how technology is enhancing the traditional role of libraries and is simultaneously forcing libraries to evolve in novel ways to meet the growing information technology expectations of the twenty-first century library patron. It also explores leading edge technologies, common problems faced by integrating such technologies and emerging trends.

Chapter 1 briefly reviews the development of libraries since antiquity and notes that they still serve the same core functions – meeting the information needs of users. Although libraries have moved from stone tablet to Kindle, our basic mission remains remarkably unchanged.

Chapter 2 introduces the role of strategic planning and establishing clear organizational goals in leveraging finite resources to meet the needs of users. Technology is expensive, and taking an inside-out approach by meeting the technology needs of librarians first is an essential key.

Chapter 3 walks through the process of finding the right fit between library and patron. We introduce needs assessment as an essential tool in ensuring your technology integration is properly aligned with the organization's strategic goals.

Chapter 4 provides an overview of current library technology, basic costs, the budgeting process and prioritization based on the strategic plan and organizational needs assessment.

Chapter 5 introduces the principles of evaluation and emphasizes the importance of a systematic, continuous evaluation process that is based on measureable targets or outcomes.

Chapter 6 explores emerging technology trends and potential implementation issues.

The goal of this book is to introduce library technology within the framework of systems design and systematic planning, in order to ensure that alignment is high between the technologies used and the users ultimately served. Libraries and information organizations continue to focus on meeting the needs of their users. In the twenty-first century, computers, the Internet and other information technologies have increasingly become the tools that libraries must use in order to adequately meet those needs.

Stone tablets, paper and the Internet: the same old library?

Abstract: Libraries have been serving users since antiquity but their purpose remains relatively unchanged – they serve the information needs of people. This chapter discusses how technology has enhanced the way libraries do what they have always done: but bigger, better and faster. Contemporary national trends of public, academic and school libraries in the US are summarized. The science of systems thinking is introduced and posited as a fundamental way in which to meet the basic information-seeking needs of people in a systematic way, and provide well-aligned resources and services that form the foundation of user services excellence.

Key words: libraries, technology, trends, user services, systems thinking, ADDIE model, information seeking, organizations, performance technology, Libraries 2.0, public, academic, school.

Libraries 2.0

Libraries are undergoing a period of incredibly rapid change. Although they continue to serve their traditional societal purpose, new technologies are allowing us to serve that purpose in bigger, better and faster ways. The genesis of the library as an intellectual repository can perhaps be traced back 32,000 years ago to when the paintings of our ancestors were created in uninhabited caves (Clottes, 2003). In ancient Mesopotamia some 5,000 years ago, thousands of clay tablets were gathered and stored in a central location and one of history's first great libraries was built in Greek Alexandria around 300 BC to house hundreds of thousands of papyrus and parchment rolls (Krasner-Khait, 2001).

In many important ways, libraries are the same as they have ever been. Growing up in the 1970s, both of us (the authors) loved going to our local libraries to spend hours exploring the stacks and using the world of books to temporarily escape the sweltering summer days of the American South. We remember comfortable chairs, bean bags, a vibrant library community and innumerable books just waiting to be discovered. Today, in 2011, we both now bring our own children to our local public libraries to do the exact same thing. The library as a safe place, a bastion of knowledge and a portal to other worlds remains unchanged. However, the transactions and efficiency, through which this takes place, have changed substantially.

As children in the 1970s we did not have personal computers or the Internet. Today, we take these tools almost for granted. Our children do not have to search a physical library catalog filled with three-by-five-inch paper index cards. In fact, they do not even have to leave home in order to peruse the holdings of our local libraries. With the online catalog, books that are already checked out are clearly marked and our children can get suggested reading lists or book reviews. Today, when we arrive at the library there are typically anywhere from 20 to 30 books waiting for us on hold at the front desk; although we still explore the stacks, most of the transaction has already taken place in an extremely effective and efficient manner.

The online environment in which our children can interact with the library changes the game. Our ability to search our public library's holdings from the comfort of our own home is both raising and shaping our children's expectations of future library services. A nationwide study of public libraries in the United States found that:

- 98.9 percent of those that responded offered free access to the Internet to patrons;
- 72.5 percent of these reported they were the only source of free Internet in their community;
- 65.2 percent offered wireless Internet;
- every Internet-based service increased. (Clark and Davis, 2009)

According to one library administrator, 'We are not being used less; we are being used differently' (Clark and Davis, 2009: 17).

Technology integration and user services

If people cannot or will not use a feature, it might as well not exist. (Nielsen and Loranger, 2006: xvi)

The central principles of usability and user-centered design are that a product or service must be high in utility and ease-of-use for the user (Nielsen, 2003). Technology is a fundamental tool for nurturing, building and delivering on this promise to users. But before we can effectively implement new technologies, we must first ascertain the needs and expectations of a typically diverse library user population.

While the expectations differ widely depending on type of library, the major components to a sound technology infrastructure can be simplified into answering one simple question – 'how strong and appropriate is your hardware and software for both your employees and the patrons?' Of course, 'strong' and 'appropriate' are subjective terms that can be answered only by your specific context. But the point is that your hardware technology infrastructure determines your capacity for delivering all other services that requires technology – and in today's wired libraries, that means virtually all of your services. Without a robust, or at least adequate, hardware infrastructure the software applications your organization needs, no matter how wonderful, will not function properly.

How does a library determine an appropriate array of information technology services and infrastructure? This book seeks to answer that question. Each semester we ask our management students, 'Which comes first, ends or means?' The answer is that ends must come first and drive the means. Librarians must use their stated ends to leverage a budget that will rarely, if ever, be as much as they need and want. Careful planning aligned to clearly identified goals is critical. Let us take a look at how to systematically plan and allocate resources accordingly.

Systems thinking and performance technology

> How can you know when you have arrived, if you have no idea where you are going? (Keller, 2000)

The underpinning process behind systems thinking is the ADDIE model, which stands for Analyse, Design, Develop, Implement and Evaluate (Clark, 2010). Utilizing this process in a formal, disciplined fashion became known as performance technology because it details an easy to understand, systematic way of achieving goals in an efficient and effective manner. Two of the pioneers of this field are close friends and colleagues, Joe Harless and Roger Kaufman. Dr Harless (1970) developed the concept of Front-End Analysis (FEA), which placed the starting point at the Analyse phase of the ADDIE model. *Analysis* of the context, goals, constraints, resources, etc. must be identified and accounted for before any proper planning could occur. Dr Kaufman (1979), however, felt that prior to analysis, one must begin at the end of the ADDIE process and *evaluate* current conditions through a formal needs assessment. In 2006, Dr. Harless finally ended this debate, which had stretched over decades, by conceding that a formal needs assessment needed to be conducted prior to analysis taking place. Figure 1.1 (Barrett, 2000) illustrates the cyclic nature of the ADDIE process.

Figure 1.2 (NOAA, 2010) shows the needs assessment as well as a more detailed breakdown of evaluation into formative (continuous, during all phases and process oriented) and summative (after implementation, output and outcome based).

We will describe how this process works within the library setting in more detail in later chapters.

Figure 1.1　ADDIE model

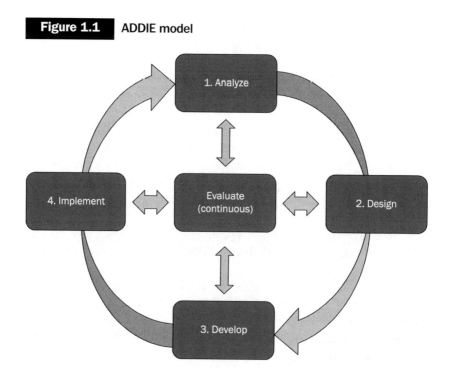

Figure 1.2 ADDIE model with needs assessment

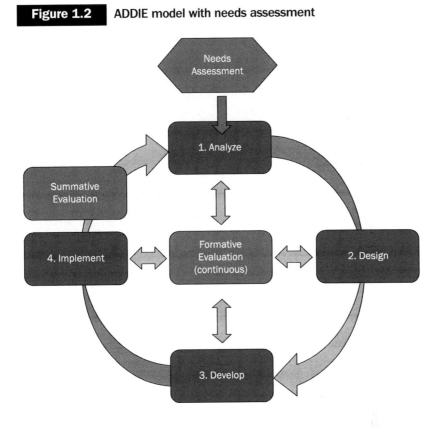

Library trends

The types of information services libraries are providing are evolving and expanding. According to an American Library Association (ALA) report, 'hard times bring libraries' value into sharper focus as the recession that took hold in December 2007 dragged on into 2010, Americans are turning to their libraries in ever larger numbers for access to resources for employment, continuing education and government services. The local library, a traditional source of free access to books, magazines, CDs and DVDs, has become a lifeline, offering technology training and workshops on topics that ranged from résumé-writing to job-interview skills' (ALA, 2010: i). Patrons are increasing their use of online job databases and career information as the federal government and other employers increasingly require that applications be completed online. In general, as demand for library services has increased, library funding has either remained static or decreased.

Public library trends

In 2010, 151.4 million Americans reported using the public library; 219 million Americans felt that the public library improved the quality of life in their community. In their communities, public libraries provide access to free Internet and 82.2 percent offer wireless environments, even in the smallest rural communities. Most are also offering homework support and classes (80 percent), virtual reference (62 percent) and e-books (55 percent). Public libraries and library staff are also important educators of technology with 53 percent reporting consistent 'point-of-use assistance' and 35 percent offering technology classes. Eighty-eight percent report having helped patrons access online job listings and other online resources, 75 percent report helping patrons with civil service exam material, 69 percent offer software or other resources that help patrons create résumés or produce other employment-related material, while 66 percent have helped patrons complete online job applications (ibid.).

The public library is most used by age groups 18–24 (80 percent reported visiting), 25–34 (70 percent reported visiting) or 35–44 (73 percent reported visiting) years old. These patrons were most likely checking out or looking for a book, an e-book or a book on tape (77 percent), consulting a librarian (67 percent), connecting to the Internet (41 percent) or checking e-mail (25 percent), especially by families for keeping in touch with defense forces overseas. Sixty percent of survey respondents renewed library resources online or via phone, 57 percent reported interacting with the library catalog either online or via phone and 42 percent reported using the library web page (ibid.).

Forty-one percent, or 61 million people, noted the top reason why they visited their public library was for educational purposes – for homework or a class. Thirty-five percent visited for entertainment purposes while 22 percent, or 33 million Americans, visited to write a paper, conduct a job search or work on a résumé. In addition, 17 percent or 26 million people visited to use the computer and an additional 11 percent visited for access to national or local news. Interestingly enough, there were also regional differences where 'Respondents in the West (27 percent) were more likely to have used library computers to write a paper or prepare a résumé than those in the Northeast (7 percent) or the South (15 percent)' (ibid.: 10). For educational purposes, 'library users in the South (50 percent) and the Northeast (48 percent) were much more likely to have visited the library ... than library users in the West (37 percent) or Midwest (28 percent)' (ibid.: 10).

Eighty-six percent of families with children of school-age reported visiting the library to access free public services such as check-out books (86 percent), read for fun (73 percent), check-out movies (46 percent), conduct research or do homework (43 percent), or attend story hour or other child-related programs (41 percent). When asked which services they would want most, 35 percent selected summer reading programs, 34 percent would like help with homework, 32 percent sought after-school programming, 28 percent wanted Story Time, 23 percent wanted computer classes and 14 percent requested teen programs (ibid.).

Academic library trends

> Even in the age of Google, academic libraries are being used more than ever. (ibid.: 19)

Despite the explosion of electronic resources available on the Internet, academic libraries are being used by students in increasingly higher numbers and are highly valued by Americans. For example, a survey conducted in 2010 (ibid.) found that 94.6 percent of students reported visiting their library's website at least once a week and nine out of ten students reported having accessed their library's online databases. In terms of the need and value of academic libraries, 95 percent or 220 million Americans felt that academic libraries served an essential role in academic learning. Information literacy is being seen as a priority student learning outcome across America's academic campuses and accrediting bodies and one of the most regularly identified metrics academic library leaders point to for validating their respective library's important strategic role on campus (Davis, 2009).

The number of e-books increased by 59.4 percent from 2006 to 2008 and total national expenditures for e-subscriptions increased from $691 million in 2006 to $1 billion in 2008. Academic librarians are also looking to explore new instructional technologies and re-evaluating how students are conducting research and learning through this process. According to Erika Linke, a past President of the Association of College and Research Libraries,

> We are educating people to learn and so we have to 'know how to know'. . . . That learning has to continue and lifelong learning skills in information technology are going to be more important than ever. Academic librarians teach students to use information resources

ethically as a stepping stone to develop their own insights and ideas – abilities that are highly prized in our entrepreneurial world (ibid.: 12).

School library trends

School libraries are also playing an increasing role in school communities – over 96 percent of Americans surveyed reported feeling that school libraries '. . . are an essential part of the education experience because they provide resources to students and teachers and because they give every child the opportunity to read and learn' (American Library Association, 2010: ii). School libraries were open 1.5 hours more per week on average in 2009 in comparison to 2008 and are spending a majority of their time playing an instructional role within the school averaging 14.5 hours per week. Visits to libraries increased by 22.7 percent for schools in the 50th percentile, 12.5 percent for schools in the 75th percentile and almost 25 percent for schools in the 95th percentile (Davis, D., 2009).

School libraries are also playing an essential role in 'keeping the digital doors open to help young people think about learning beyond the classroom' (ALA, 2010: ii). School library collections also continue to grow, with increases in books, periodicals subscriptions and video and audio materials. In addition, computers with network access increased cumulatively by 27 percent from 2008 to 2010. English Language Learners (ELL) also comprised 14 percent of the respondents to the 'Schools Library Count!' national survey, which reported having a study body comprised of 25 percent or more of ELL students. One in every five elementary schools (19 percent) reported having a study population of 25 percent or more ELL students (ibid.).

Foundations of information seeking and user services in information organizations

He comes to the library or information center as one of several possible alternatives, for information to fill out 'his picture of the world'. (Taylor, 1968: 178)

Before a user seeks information they must have a need; according to Taylor this need reflects a user's desire to ease a 'vague sense of dissatisfaction' (as cited in Case, 2007: 72). This dissatisfaction fuels a cognitive inquiry path involving four steps:

- establishes a tangible need (visceral);
- that becomes a need that is attenuated to (conscious);
- constructs and articulates a concrete need that should be addressed (formal);
- and finally, a negotiation takes place between information seeker and available sources to identify the most appropriate path towards meeting the need (compromised).

This final stage where the information seeker selects an initial pathway is the entry point into an initial communication with an information system or service provider (Taylor, 1968).

Belkin, Oddy and Brooks (1982) describe a user's information need as a '. . . recognized anomaly in the user's state of knowledge concerning some topic or situation and that, in general, the user is unable to specify precisely what is needed to resolve that anomaly'. Derwin describes this information need as 'sense-making' of a gap in knowledge that needs filling (Case, 2007). Users seek information to meet an information need and this process is highly unique, contextualized and constructivist in nature (Morris, 1994). Often information seekers arrive at the reference desk seeking help for an information need they have not formulated well yet.

Pirolli and Card take a behavioural and biological approach to information seeking through their information foraging theory – referred to as the adaptive control of thought in information foraging (ACT-IF) model that posits humans are informavores (Denis, 1991, as cited in Pirolli and Card, 1999) on the hunt for the information they seek. Information seeking behavior pathways help shape the information systems being used where, '. . . when feasible, natural information systems evolve toward stable states that maximize gains of valuable information per unit cost (*see also* Resnikoff, 1989: 97). Cognitive systems engaged in information foraging will exhibit such adaptive tendencies' (Pirolli and Card, 1999: 643). Those developing information architectures for digital and online information searching seek to develop clear and strong 'information scents' so that users can find what they are looking for as efficiently and effectively as possible (Morville and Rosenfield, 2008).

The next step in the information seeking process involves an emotional and affective stage where the information seeker braves the potential fear of 'asking a stupid question' and approaches someone to help them answer their questions. Remember though, often this question is not well formulated, so the information seeking process will need help on several levels. The first is on the emotional and personal level involving non-verbal communication (NVC). When someone is looking for help, they rely heavily on the non-verbal body language of the service provider through eye contact, facial expressions and body posture. Some researchers claim NVC comprises over 90 percent of the entire communication transaction (Fromkin and Rodman, 1983 as cited in Gabbott and Hogg, 2001).

Richmond et al. (1991, as cited in Gabbott and Hogg, 2001) posit there are six primary inter-related functions involved in non-verbal communication:

- repeat or reinforce a verbal message (I'm here to help you or you are bothering me);
- a substitute for verbal communication (please come ask me a question or I'm busy now);
- an accent or emphasis to a verbal message (that's a great question or are you kidding me?);
- contradict a verbal message (words say how can I help you while the body is saying I'm not interested in what you are saying);
- regulate the social exchange (a pause and eye contact suggest it is the other person's turn to speak);
- it reflects emotions behind the words (I'm really excited about helping you or you are bothering me and I'm not really interested in helping you so please go away).

Ramsey and Sohi (1997, as cited in Commer and Drollinger, 1999) suggest that this verbal and non-verbal communication exchange occurs within the context of three phases of listening:

- sensing (I understand what you are saying);
- processing (I am thinking about what you are saying);
- responding (I am letting you know I understand).

The quality in which someone is *really* listening can also be broken down into:

- *marginal listening* (you are listening but you really are not hearing or processing the information because you are thinking about something else);
- *evaluative listening* (you are hearing what is being said but either not understanding it or not letting the speaker know you are understanding it through either verbal or non-verbal communication);

- *active listening* (you get it and let them know, both verbally and non-verbally, that you get it) (Alessandra et al., 1987, as cited in Commer and Drollinger, 1999).

Tsai (2001, as cited in Yuksel, 2008: 58) in fact found that, 'employee smiling and eye contact were related to the customers' greater willingness to revisit the store and to pass on complimentary comments about the store to friends'.

Some researchers (Mattila, 2001, as cited in Yuksel, 2008) suggest that customers of any service ascertain the overall quality of a service exchange on three criteria:

- *outcome* (how much did they benefit from the exchange);
- *procedure* (the degree in which the organization's policies and method of dealing with the issue was satisfactory);
- *interaction* (the overall interpersonal treatment during the interaction).

The affective state of the service provider, '. . . such as their friendliness, responsiveness and enthusiasm – have been argued to exert a positive influence on customers' overall evaluation of service consumption experiences and perceptions of service quality' (Elizur, 1987 and Sundaram and Webster, 2000, as cited in Yuksel, 2008). Empirical evidence suggests that non-verbal cues play a significant role in shaping receivers' perceptions of communicators' credibility, persuasive power, courtesy and interpersonal warmth' (Sundaram and Webster, 2000, as cited in Yuksel, 2008: 60).

Within the specific realm of technology support and user services in a library, however, additional dynamics are introduced. Both the user and information service provider may lack confidence in their technological expertise. Users may be especially reluctant to seek help because of fears that they do not know enough to ask an intelligent question in case they appear incompetent. The fear of rejection when someone seeks help is referred to as one's perceived threat (Fisher et al., 1981 and Karabenick and Knapp, 1991, as cited in Kitsantas and Chow, 2007), which reflects a fear of the impact the transaction may have on their self-esteem.

One of the authors used to manage a technology support desk staffed by young, bright information technology students. Help-seekers included faculty, staff and students of a large LIS program. Our young staff, however, were not naturally inclined to provide very good customer service because they focused primarily on the technology. Although they were very knowledgeable and confident in their technology support abilities, those who sought help from our unit traditionally were not. This introduced a power imbalance that typically is present in all customer/employee transactions but is magnified in technology support. Help-seekers would enter our help-desk area and our staff, busily working on another technology problem, would be too focused to even stop and make eye contact.

In order to address this problem, we developed the Analyze, Identify and Resolve (AIR) model to serve as a conceptual framework to guide the technology support interaction. The *Analyze* phase involved active listening (high verbal and non-verbal cues) to the user that also allowed for some level of venting by the user as they were invariably frustrated when they approached us. This venting period was invaluable for two reasons – the help-seeker would be able to release some of her/his frustration and the help-provider would be able to better understand the specific context in which the problem was occurring. The *Identify* phase involved exploring a number of potential scenarios by thoroughly listening to and interacting with the help-seeker to be sure our understanding of the technical problem was correct. Once we were clear to the best of the help-seeker's knowledge what the problem was, a solution that had the highest likelihood of success could be identified and offered as a potential course of action. The *Resolution* process addressed the need to address the help-seeker's problem on both a short-term and long-term basis. Often, the need was urgent (i.e. instructional technology was not working or a printer was jammed) and the short-term fix was to just help the user with another projector or print out her/his grant proposal at the help-desk and then work on the longer-term fix of repairing the technology problem. Before we developed this service model, our IT staff would try and fix the IT problem, without comprehending that the user really was less concerned about the technology malfunction itself and was much more concerned about obtaining their desired end result as quickly as possible. The last critical component of the *Resolution* phase was to be sure that any issue that could not be immediately fixed was entered in as a technology support ticket so that staff across shifts would be able to work on the issue and to ensure that it was not forgotten.

From an organizational level, Blanchard and Bowles (1993) noted that exemplary customer service can only be realized if quality extended beyond a singular transaction with a specific employee and is instead institutionalized, so that excellence in customer service is consistent, flexible and personal for both the employees and the customer. In terms of service excellence, Kem Ellis (21 March 2011), High Point Public, NC

Library Director for 20 years, noted that 'the most successful employees are the ones who are living in service for something larger than themselves'. He further points out that these employees understand how their work applies to the bigger picture and is directly contributing to the success of the users they serve. His organization's top strategic priority in fact states, 'grow more loyal promoters'. The message for all members of the library is that if visitors have a positive 'memorable experience' they will promote the library to other potential patrons.

Cynthia Curtis, Media Coordinator at Hanes Magnet School in Winston Salem, NC, mentions that providing customer service for middle-school teachers and students is all about her personal connection with each of them and meeting them at their point of need. She conscientiously seeks to remember everyone by first name and states she '... listens and understands where they are and then communicates where I am', which is a fluid process so they both are on the same page (Davis, C., 2011).

Sandy Neerman (2011), Director of Greensboro, NC, Public Libraries, has a particular message for those who seek to serve in libraries:

> So many times people come into our profession and do not understand that ... everything is about serving. And doing that from the day you first walk in the door to the day you retire. . . . And it makes no difference what product you are delivering or what the customer asks. . . . Often we get folks that become interested in our profession because of what it represents philosophically and what we are as an institution but forget we are to serve everybody . . . the richest to poorest, the smartest to the people that can't read, to the people that look nice and the people that come in here and are hard to stand beside because of their aroma. . . . This comes as a shock at times for people.

University-wide research at our own local institution shows that users prefer virtual means to answer basic factual questions (Google, information from the library website, or virtual reference such as e-mail or online chat) but still prefer face-to-face help for more complex research questions (Chow and Croxton, 2011). While examination of the various cognitive, personal and communication theories involved in a user/service provider interaction shows how complex it actually is, in the end, Blanchard and Bowles (1993) keep it elegantly simple: exemplary customer service is all about people meeting the needs of other people. If those providing the information services genuinely are committed to serving those seeking help, regardless of appearance, level of knowledge, or type of question, then the user-services transaction will most likely be a success.

Pulling it all together

Despite the proliferation of Internet access and usage nationally, our public, academic and school libraries are being used more than ever. One could surmise that instead of replacing libraries, access to the Internet has led to expanded library use as patrons are able to remotely access an expanded suite of online information and services such as Online Public Access Catalogs (OPAC), proprietary databases, information on programming, digital content and virtual reference services. Public libraries are offering far more than books as patrons turn to them for computing and Internet access, education, entertainment and job-related material. Academic libraries are also increasingly involved in education (particularly in teaching information literacy to faculty and students), are heavily investing in e-subscriptions to online content and are providing innovative collaborative and group study environments. School libraries are also spending the majority of time in instructionally related activities while serving as an educational resource for the entire learning community.

When looking at all three types of libraries, it is clear that there is a heavy emphasis on technology and education and that libraries are continuing to serve as bastions of knowledge for the communities they serve. The seminal questions to be explored in this book are who are the users of libraries and what kinds of technology are needed to meet their information and educational needs? Chapter 2 will detail how to apply the ADDIE model and needs assessment, to help create a strategic plan that will clearly identify what technology is needed to achieve specified, high priority ends.

Strategic planning, organizational goals and technology: what and for whom?

Abstract: Where does one begin in deciding what technology is best for one's library? The close alignment between organizational and user goals is critical in identifying and implementing the appropriate technology solutions. This chapter walks step-by-step through the process of conducting a needs assessment and developing a strategic plan, and discusses the relationship between following the process and creating a world-class working environment for employees and users alike. Readers are provided with a blue-print for how to develop one on their own. Once a strategic plan is created that paints the strategic goals of both the organization and the users it hopes to serve, the appropriate technology to facilitate attainment of these goals can then be identified.

Key words: strategic planning, needs assessment, vision statement, mission statement, values, core competencies, SMART goals, goals and objectives, user services, world class.

Technology is expensive, requires frequent maintenance and becomes outdated quickly. Selecting the appropriate technology based on the needs of users and the organization is critical. Technology is a means not an end. The 'need', a collective term for the fundamental ways in which various users utilize the organization's goods and services, represents the ultimate organizational 'ends'. Defining clear ends is paramount to ensuring precious, limited budgets are allocated as efficiently and effectively as possible. The ADDIE systems design model represents a robust systems approach to ensuring organizational goals are clear, accurate and aligned to both user and funding agency goals.

Utilizing the ADDIE model as a framework (Analyze, Design, Develop, Implement and Evaluate) (Clark, 2010), three major organizational planning tools can be implemented in a systematic, step-wise fashion – needs assessment, strategic planning and budgeting. As discussed in Chapter 1, Joe Harless finally conceded that the needs assessment must be the first step in the 'A' or Analyze stage, the first step in the ADDIE process.

Needs assessment

Assessing needs is a straightforward concept. But conducting one that is valid, reliable and current is difficult. We view this as a four step process:

- determine whose need actually should be identified;
- assess the need by communicating with each constituency group using multiple methods;
- collect statistics around existing resources and usage patterns (i.e. circulation history, computer usage, etc.);
- analyse the results and create a priority list of each group's goals.

These analyses and identified goals serve as the foundation for beginning the second phase of the ADDIE process, the 'D' or Design phase.

Whose needs should be considered and assessed? Kaufman's Organizational Elements Model (OEM) (Kaufman et al., 2001) holds that there are three primary needs any organization must consider: Mega (societal); Macro (external to the organization); and Micro (organizational). The mega level views society as the primary customer or stakeholder of any organization's goods and services; the value added by an organization represents the goals of society or the local community that the organization resides in. The macro level represents the organizational goals of the parent or funding agency. The micro goals are the specific goals of the organization itself. The need – expressed in the form of specific, measurable goals – of all three organizational levels should be aligned.

Step 1

At each of the three levels there are influential people, documents and stakeholders that should be consulted. The mega or community level for academic libraries, for example, might be taking a look at community (even national or international) priorities in terms of economic development, quality of life and research emphasis of faculty and students. For school libraries the mega level might focus on parents, employers and community leaders that can answer the question, 'What should our children and students be able to do with what they are learning in school?' and, more importantly, 'How can school libraries help with this?' For public libraries, the mega level certainly could be helped to be defined by local community citizens of all ages, leaders (i.e. board of supervisors or commissioners, etc.) and state and local trends.

The macro level reflects the external environment that has a direct impact on that organization's goals (i.e. the priorities of those funding the organization) and should be directly linked to previously identified mega goals. For academic libraries, this certainly would involve, at minimum, the goals and priorities for a state-level governing body (for public) or corporation (for private) and then hierarchically work its way down to the university, the university's leadership and also any Friends of the Library boards. For school libraries, this would also start at minimum with state-level educational priorities as well as the local board of education and superintendent and then within the school itself, school administration and PTA. For public libraries, certainly again at minimum start at the state-level bodies that are helping shape the goals of the state as well as local governing bodies such as the city council or board of supervisors, mayor and Friends of the Library.

Understanding the larger contexts of mega and macro will help the organization properly align its own goals (micro) to the priority goals of society and its primary users, as well as those of relevant local governing bodies and primary funders. While it may initially appear that such an approach may too rigidly limit creativity and autonomy, ultimately it helps ensure that the larger goals of the organization's environment are known and understood. While aligning organizational priorities to those of larger constituencies makes intuitive sense, commitment to this process is up to the discretion of the organization.

Step 2

Once the core constituencies are identified, step two in the process is discovering their needs in a valid, reliable fashion. Obviously, asking them directly is easiest to do, but how does one most appropriately do that? Interviews with 'power' users – high-level decision-makers (that help establish large-scale visions but may not know much about frontline operations) represent one essential point of data. Collecting documentation that articulates mission and vision statements and priority goals is a second seminal piece of information. Learning directly from the primary users of your organization through interviews, focus groups, natural observation and surveys is also essential. A key aspect to remember is that such discovery usually will not be for research purposes so the pressure of having to implement a perfectly valid survey, focus group, or set of interview questions should be alleviated to a large extent. Gathering data, as potentially invalid and non-generalizable as it may be, will still help more clearly understand need at mega and macro contexts than with no data at all; the process itself in this case is the most important.

Nevertheless, it is important to keep in mind that each constituency will have its own unique perspective on user needs and that no one group can accurately speak for all. For example, the most frequently consulted group are the public services staff, because they are the library employees with the most direct contact with the public and should arguably thus be the most aware of user needs. But that group is typically too intimately aware of the library's services and resources to be able to truly see things from a user viewpoint and they tend to interact with a very small percentage of the overall user population. Users are sometimes consulted during the needs analysis phase. One might assume that this group would be able to give relatively accurate assessments of their own needs, but that isn't always the case. A few years ago, we conducted user surveys in several library instruction classes. We asked our students, 'Would you use chat reference if we offered it?' and an overwhelming percentage answered in the affirmative. But when we implemented the service, only a very small percentage actually utilized it. In this case, there was a tremendous gap between those who thought they would use it and those that actually did. It is important to keep in mind that surveys, focus groups and interviews test perceptions – and that those perceptions may not always match up with reality.

Of course, there is another significant reason to ask people what they want; any effective action plan will need the buy-in and cooperation of multiple groups. Those groups will be most enthusiastic if they feel they have had a meaningful opportunity to provide input.

Step 3

The subjective opinions of varying groups provide valuable information, but are best used when combined with more objective usage data.

Fortunately, most libraries keep copious amounts of usage data in the forms of server log files, service desk statistics, circulation data and various usage statistics for electronic resources. This data can be used to make decisions about which services have the highest priority. For example, if the users are flocking to a library's e-journals and the use of printed journals is in serious decline, then the library might want to consider moving some money from the print to electronic format. The great benefit of this approach is that you can base your priorities on what people actually use, as opposed to their subjective opinion of what they might want to use in the future. The problem with this approach is that it measures only quantity of use and ignores quality of use and that can be misleading. For example, web log files could tell a library that their electronic books page is the most frequently visited page on the site. From that, one might infer that people love the e-book collection and think the service is wonderful. But the numbers don't actually say that. It may well be that the users are looking for the Library Catalog and click on an 'Electronic Books' web link because they think it is an electronic way to find printed books. Or they may be looking for particular e-books and not finding them. Or, perhaps most frustrating of all, they might find exactly the e-book they want, but then not be able to figure out how to read or check it out online. So, the fact that people use a service a lot does not by itself prove that the service is successful.

Step 4

If neither subjective survey data nor objective usage data gives a complete picture, then how can we ever trust data to effectively inform our decision making? The answer lies in the use of multiple approaches. This is referred to as data triangulation – multiple perspectives and data points of the same phenomenon help create a rich, authentic picture from the viewpoints of different constituents. Ideally, libraries gather information from informal communications and more formal interviews, focus groups, surveys and statistics that indicate the major goals of both the external and internal environment and also show how the library is currently being used (or how similar libraries are being used). That information can then be used to begin establishing the library's information technology priorities. The points where 'what is expected' and 'what is' diverge are called the gaps or unmet need that should be addressed.

Now that some general goals have been identified the key is to list each group's priorities in rank order and then compare them to one another in preparation for listing them in a strategic plan. It is critical that each group's results are looked at separately first so that all of the time and effort spent collecting the results can be looked at with face value within each group. List a top-five and up to a top-ten set of goals for each group. Once you have these goals then it is time to determine which of them are appropriate to work on for your organization.

Before we begin our discussion on strategic planning, let us first define 'goal' and consider how best to write one. According to the *Merriam-Webster Dictionary* (n.d.(a)), a goal is defined as 'the end toward which effort is directed'. In other words, goals represent the end that an organization would like to achieve; these ends, however, can be articulated as verb-driven actions or noun-driven accomplishments. Which is best?

On one hand, many people prefer goals articulated with action-oriented verbs. So, for example, if the mega-level societal goal is articulated as 'creating a high quality of life for all citizens' it is action-oriented through the use of the verb *creating*, focused on achieving *a high quality of life for all citizens*. The potential danger, however, is that too much attention could be focused on the process and act of 'creating' as opposed to actually achieving 'a high quality of life'. Is the ultimate desired outcome the act of doing something or the end state of accomplishment that result from the action?

In the performance technology world, goals are often stated as nouns and accomplishments (ends achieved with high quality) (Harless, 1998). So in our example, the goal would be simply stated as *a high quality of life for all citizens*. The entire focus of this goal is on achieving such an end and not on the process for getting there.

Strategic planning

> Long-range planning does not deal with future decisions, but with the future of present decisions. (Peter Drucker, as cited in Bolt and Stephan, 1998: 1)

A strategic plan is more than just a document; it reflects a meeting place of thoughts, ideas and perspectives of an entire organization. The process of putting together a plan is in many ways just as important as the goals it ultimately identifies – individual perspectives are asked for, shared, heard, considered and then, ideally, processed together to form a concrete vision for the future of the organization. The result of the process is an organization united in its collective vision.

In general, a strategic plan has five major components

- a mission statement
- a vision statement
- organizational values
- core competencies
- priority organizational goals and objectives.

A mission statement is the organization's rallying cry; it can be used on a day-to-day basis to guide and inspire members of the organization. This is not easy and many mission statements are mocked and disregarded because they are neither meaningful nor relevant to employees, some of whom may have had little or no say during the creation of the statement. In order to encourage buy-in and to keep the document fresh, the mission statements and the entire strategic plan should be revisited frequently for relevance, timeliness and accomplishments (annually or bi-annually). There is no minimum length for a good mission statement; some are a brief, concise sentence and some are a collection of sentences that form themselves into inspiring paragraphs. The key is to capture the essence of your organization in a statement or set of statements that represents the bottom line of the organization, which usually is a mega end.

The vision statement reflects what the organization wishes for the future. Similar to a mission statement, the significant difference resides in scope and focus – whereas the mission statement reflects the purpose of the organization in relatively concrete goals, the vision statement focuses more on an idealistic vision for the future. Although both should be inspiring, the mission focuses on the day-to-day while the vision focuses on the future.

The values establish the work culture and represent discussion points and expectations around day-to-day rules of engagement between members of the organization as well as with external customers. While professional standards such as *trust and communication, integrity, a team of one* and *passion for customers* are intuitive, having a discussion as an organization on which ones are the most important, and also what each mean operationally, is critical. Remember that new members join your organization frequently and ensuring that they have an opportunity to articulate their own meaning of what is important to them and understand the collective values of the organization is essential; it is a two-way street and not something that simply can be 'trained' or thrust into them by the organization.

Core competencies reflect the organization's most useful and valued skill sets. While it is tempting to say 'everything', resources are always limited, and having a priority list is important both in terms of strategic focus (You only have so much time in a day, week, month, year) and budgetary priorities (What are you going to spend your money on? What does not get funded?). Once these competencies are identified, they can serve as a foundation for the organization's strategic and priority goals and objectives. Clearly, these should be aligned with the identified core competencies – how do you become stronger in your priority areas of competency? To do so you must be aware of what they are first.

Priority goals and objectives are the last and most significant part of a strategic plan. There are three primary ways to help determine what these goals should be:

1. The goals are often mapped directly to higher level organizational strategic plans on the macro and mega levels. Ideally, your organization's priority goals will align with those who are ultimately funding the organization.

2. SWOT analysis – this organizational tool involves an informal look at an organization's Strengths, Weaknesses, Opportunities and Threats. Examining these four areas for an organization will allow the identification of a long list of goals that need to be addressed in the future.

3. An organizational retreat that reviews results from a needs assessment to ensure that the needs of all major stakeholders of the organization are accounted for and included in the organizational goals.

When considering a SWOT analysis, it is important to remember that not all issues in each of the four areas can be addressed at the same time, but it does allow the organization the clarity of vision to decide what needs to be accomplished in the future given its present reality. While determining which goals should be addressed first, an organization can choose to focus more on its strengths and opportunities (an offensive posture) or its weaknesses and threats (a defensive posture); another way to frame this question is, 'Do you want to become more of who you already are or more of what you are currently not?' Arguably, a good course of action would be to build on your organizational strengths and opportunities while shoring up major gaps and ensuring major threats are accounted for. The focus, however, is on becoming more of what your organization is already, thereby building on what you already have, as opposed to shifting too much time and resources towards addressing weaknesses and threats as the organization's primary goals. It is especially important that alignment occurs between the desired strengths of the organization and the given strengths and unique talents of the people who work for your organization. A mismatch would cause serious gaps in the organization's ability to meet its future goals.

As discussed above, a goal can be written as a verb or a noun. Regardless of which way you choose, a goal represents a future, measurable end that is to be attained. Articulating this clearly allows the organization to then identify and allocate resources that represent explicitly marked pathways to those ends. Given finite amounts of time and resources, an organization can only have so many priority goals to achieve if it is to attain any of them with any level of quality. Keep in mind that each goal must also have several objectives, sub-steps to achieving the ultimate end; a good rule of thumb is three to five goals maximum. Any more than that and the organization runs the risk of over-extending itself and not accomplishing any of them. Having more than five also suggests that you have not prioritized your goals in rank order and that there are too many 'high' priorities to practically achieve with any level of quality. Remember, these are the priorities you will focus on achieving strategically through allocating organizational resources. Focusing on too many at one time will dilute your resources and increase the likelihood of not having enough resources to accomplish any or most of them.

A guideline for writing quality goals is to use the mnemonic SMART or goals that are Specific, Measurable, Attainable, Realistic and Timely (SMART Goals, 2010). Some also follow the acronym SMARTER goals by adding an 'E' for Exciting and/or Ethical and an 'R' for Realistic and/or Resources (available) to the end of SMART. This guideline reinforces the need to make organizational goals achievable.

Each priority goal identified represents an accomplishment that will be a sum of its total parts. These parts or sub-steps represent the objectives that must be achieved in order for the goal itself to be achieved. Whereas the goal is a high-level, more general goal, the objectives are more narrowly defined stepping stones on the path towards where you want to go. Let us use an example starting with a goal of updating a library collection.

The goal can be stated either as a noun, 'a relevant library collection', or a process with a verb, 'making the library collection more relevant'. The former views the goal as past-tense and a goal that *has been achieved*; the latter is more action oriented and present-tense and a goal that *is being achieved*. Let us go with the noun-based, accomplished goal of 'a relevant library collection'. Is this a SMART goal? Specific – yes. Measurable – not yet but will be covered in the objectives. Attainable – not yet but again will be covered in the objectives. Realistic – not yet but again should be addressed in the objectives. Timely – this also will be handled in the objectives. How about Exciting/Ethical – this would be our first 'no' as the word 'relevant' is not too exciting. How about Realistic/Resources – again we cannot tell right now without writing the objectives. At this juncture we are still not sure if our goal abides by either the SMART or SMARTER guideline and we have a big 'no' in terms of whether it is exciting. Let us spice it up a bit and change the goal from 'a relevant library collection' to 'a vibrant, user-centered collection'.

Let us call our new goal, goal number one and write it simply as: 'Goal 1: A vibrant, user-centered collection'.

The objectives of this goal would be the stepping stones towards achieving it. These objectives should be written as subparts to the goal. So in order to achieve this goal, a library might identify the following specific, measurable objectives:

Goal 1: a vibrant, user-centered collection

Objective 1.1: hold user advisory focus groups by March 2011.
Objective 1.2: prepare collection development plan by June 2011.
Objective 1.3: seek 30 percent increase in collection budget for 2011–2012 fiscal year.

The objectives represent the steps towards achieving the goal; small, incremental steps that as a whole might appear overwhelming and unrealistic. Setting concrete, achievable goals that can be measured allows the organization to specifically measure its progress. Even if the ultimate goal is not achieved (yet) the organization is able to measure tangibly how close it actually is. Each year the organization's set of goals and each goal's respective objectives should be revisited to determine progress, relevancy and whether each should remain in the organization's top five or so high-priority goals. These goals or ends the organization is trying to achieve reflect what and how its resources should be allocated. This means they drive the budget, which will be covered in Chapter 4.

Strategic planning and world-class user services

Happy employees make happy customers. In a landmark 25-year study conducted by the Gallup Organization (Buckingham and Coffey, 1999), the secrets for how some of the world's top organizations were managed were revealed. The book, entitled *First, Break All the Rules*, focuses on 12 key factors, all of which center on the employees themselves; when an organization creates a positive work environment that allows their employees to answer 'yes' to each of the 12 questions, that organization is rewarded with higher productivity, happier customers and had higher retention (Buckingham and Coffman, 1999). To satisfy your users, you must first satisfy your employees.

How does this relate to strategic planning and technology? Of the 12 questions, seven can be tied directly to an organization's strategic plan (all 12 can be tied indirectly) and whether an employee would be able to answer 'yes' or 'no'. The key components are: does the employee know what they are expected to do on a daily basis (Q1); do they have the necessary material and resources to do this job well (Q2); and are their assigned tasks a good fit for their strengths and what they like to do (Q3)? In addition, strategic planning also helps to allow employees a strategic voice in what the organizational goals are and how they are to be achieved (Q7); general resonance and buy-in of the organizational goals through helping craft and approve the organization's mission statement (Q8); a sense of confidence that co-workers are similarly invested and their work is contributing to the bottom line (Q9); and that there is a sense of friendship and a common bond among employees towards achieving a united purpose (Q10) (ibid.).

Another classic management theory is Blanchard and Bowles's *Raving Fans* (1993), which suggests that, rather than seeking satisfied customers, organizations should seek to create 'raving' fans of the organization. Through three interdependent strategies – Decide (what you want), Discover (what the customer wants) and Deliver +1 (improve in small, strategic increments) – the organization can clearly define its goals, vet them with customers or users and then move strategically forward towards accomplishing these goals with high degrees of quality and consistency. The central tenet of this theory is that organizations must focus on a small set of concrete goals and then maintain a consistent focus on achieving them. Organizations and employees cannot be all things to all people. A lack of organizational focus typically leads to spreading money and resources too thinly, risking failure of many initiatives, high stress levels for employees and lower customer satisfaction levels. Organizations should under-promise and over-deliver. When this is done consistently, employees and customers become 'raving fans', eager to spread the word about the merits of your organization. In the end, however, the greatest key to success is just remembering that providing a product or service is all about people (employees) meeting the needs of people (customers), and that it is the human connection and exchange around the actual transaction that is most important. People want to know that their needs and desires are understood, validated and met with a high level of respect, integrity and sincerity.

For a library in the 21st century it is tempting to try and be 'all things to all people' as the potential constituencies and the ways they can access and use library services become more diverse. To attempt to do this, however, at the expense of clear, consistent and strategic organizational goals would be putting the organization on tenuous ground in terms of having the necessary resources to meet rapidly changing and divergent needs. Core competencies of the organization and core groups of users must be identified so that strategic goals and limited resources can be brought to bear to realize them in a consistent, workman-like fashion. Technology, above all else, is one of the greatest resources that can be utilized in helping achieve organizational goals.

Creating a strategic plan

The design and development of a strategic plan involves the entire organization. This can be an intimidating and overwhelming idea but the key is to identify and answer questions about the organization in five main areas:

- Vision (for the future);
- Mission (organizational action statement);
- Values (cultural underpinnings and ethical foundation);
- Competencies (core products and services);
- Goals and Objectives.

Let us walk through a step-by-step example.

Step 1: what do you want to be when you grow up?

Before you can establish the vision for the future and a mission statement that serves as a rallying cry that will inspire everyone in the organization, it is critical to adhere to Raving Fan Secret #1 and *Decide What You Want*. In other words, what is your organization good at and what does it want to become and for whom? Keep in mind that to attempt to be all things to all people will limit your organization's ability to focus finite resources on a few concrete goals thereby increasing the likelihood of not being great at anything. What are the three to five products and/or services your organization wants to focus on and what users are being served?

Let us pick a typical metropolitan downtown public library to use as an example. This public library has a diverse user population comprised primarily of the business sector, the homeless and indigent, general walk-in public and families with youth. Statistics suggest that usage of career resources and reference requests in this area has been continuously increasing over the past two years. In addition, the homeless and indigent population has continued to increase in number, although outside of the physical use of the lobby and restroom facilities, actual use of electronic and collection resources is minimal. The library also has a strong core of youth users and their family as the city's cultural center is nearby and a steady stream of families are always present in the library. Can the library cater to all three constituents equally?

A closer look at the data shows that the use of the library's electronic resources and databases from the web have continued to increase exponentially while patrons physically visiting the library appear to be largely in the homeless and indigent group or the family and youth group. From a core competency standpoint, the library could then choose the following to prioritize both in terms of time and resources:

1. quality online services and resources;
2. career resources and services;
3. support for the homeless and indigent population;
4. youth and family services.

An important reminder is that an organizational retreat would be the appropriate manner to discuss and build a strategic plan. It is critical that all members of the organization are provided with an opportunity to provide input and their perspective into this process. While preliminary work on the strategic plan by the library's management is appropriate it is, while easy to do, inappropriate to not include the entire organization in discussing, contributing to (and buying into) the organizational plan, especially since the majority of the staff will be in charge of actual day-to-day implementation with patrons. Without buy-in and feedback, the organization would have the stereotypical mission and organizational goals thrust down from above, which is usually summarily ignored and tolerated at best.

Now that the library's core competencies are clear and aligned to specific user groups, it is time to develop both a vision statement, which is a vision for what the organization hopes to become in the future, and a mission statement, which is a statement of action designed to both inspire and ground members of the organization to the organization's values, goals and objectives in their day-to-day work. Both should be clear and articulate enough to help members of the organization be able to, at a glance, understand how their work is contributing to the organization in the present and future.

Step 2: developing vision and mission statements

In our example, the public library has identified four core competencies centered on its primary users and the growing trends occurring around it that suggest the need of these users will increase in the future. An appropriate vision statement that is concise, inspiring and to the point might be, *One city, one people; serving the community is a privilege and our passion*. Such a statement captures a call to public service with a strategic focus on meeting the needs of patrons and doing so with passion and commitment for all members of the constituency, disparate as they may be. It is also action oriented and concise enough to appear as a tag line on letter head, posters, flyers, etc.

The mission statement is a statement of action for the present, day-to-day activities of the organization and should share similar traits to the vision statement: short, concise, inspiring and a uniting statement (note we did not say dry and boring) for all members of the organization. Keep in mind that the need for such a mission statement is primarily to energize and inspire action or to help employees stay focused in potentially trying, confusing times (i.e. when dealing with a disgruntled patron, experiencing budget cuts, disagreeing with co-workers, etc.). A potential mission statement for our exemplar library would be, *We are your partners in providing world class resources and compassionate service you want and need*. Such a mission statement embraces collaboration through the use of the word 'we' and emphasizes personalized services that are designed around the user base the library has identified as its major constituency. In addition, the rallying cry is not merely providing services but 'world class' resources and 'compassionate' services, which encourages attention to delivering day-to-day services with excellence, respect and caring.

One key reminder at this stage of the process is that not everyone will initially agree on any of the items just discussed and described. More importantly, as you work through such a process you will not agree with everything. Compromise is a must and incorporating input from everyone is vital for the process to truly work and empower everyone in the organization. It is in fact this disagreement and required work towards compromise that helps bring the organization together.

Step 3: establishing your cultural foundation – organizational values

Determining organizational values helps provide members with a lens through which to view their everyday activities. It also helps people stay true to what is most important when the going gets tough. Without well-articulated values it is more difficult for members of the organization to be on the same page and approach similar tasks within similar frameworks. This leads to inconsistencies that will be explicitly apparent, especially to users.

For our library, the mission and vision statements establish a clear path that organizational values need to support:

- *Mission statement*: 'We are your partners in providing world class resources and compassionate service you want and need.'
- *Vision statement*: 'One city, one people; serving the community is a privilege and our passion.'

Keep in mind as well that research supports the notion that employees well taken care of, and flourishing employees, are the foundation for delivering consistently excellent services to customers and users. The organizational values of our library might look something like:

- Value 1: Excellence in all that we do
  - +1 percent service comes from treating people like a real, unique person and not someone you are merely serving.
  - Do everything with quality.
  - Remember the platinum rule – treat others as they want to be treated.
  - Achieve excellence through consistency and delivering on what we promise.
- Value 2: Trust and communication
  - Do what you say you are going to do.

- Let people know when you are not happy with things.
- Communicate openly and without fear.
- Ensure disagreements are resolved through clear, candid communication and understanding.
- Trust that we all honor and respect one another in all things that we do.

■ Value 3: Honor and integrity
  - Respect yourself and others equally.
  - Honor patrons as they are and not how we wish they would be.
  - Treat patrons with integrity by meeting them at their point of need with validation and compassion.
  - Apply the Platinum Rule: Treat others as they wish to be treated.

When writing values, define and operationalize them by providing examples of how the value might be applied throughout the organization. Now that we have established the core competencies, vision and mission statement and the organization's core cultural values, we are ready to establish high priority goals and objectives that are tightly aligned to the organization's vision of its present and future.

Step 4: establishing goals and objectives

Within the contextual framework established by the previous three steps, we are now ready to establish goals and objectives that operationalize what the organization would like to achieve. For our public library the goals and objectives should be prioritized around its primary users and meeting their needs within the context of its stated four core competencies – quality online services, career resources and services, supporting the homeless and indigent population and youth and family services. Another decision point is whether to continue building on the organization's existing strengths or focus on making weak areas stronger.

The core competencies serve as a logical set of goals and objectives that can be articulated in the form of accomplished goals (nouns) rather than statements of action (verbs):

Goal 1: quality online services and resources
Goal 2: comprehensive career resources and services

Goal 3: multi-faceted services and support for the homeless and indigent population

Goal 4: world class youth and family collection and services.

Each goal is mapped directly to the organization's articulated core competencies. There should be several objectives, cobblestones that form the pathway to attaining the goal, that are identified and assigned an approximate ETA or estimated time of accomplishment. Standard strategic goals focus on a three to five year time period. Let us address each of the four goals.

Goal 1: quality online services and resources

- Objective 1.1: bi-annual needs assessments of patrons and non-users (every November, April);
- Objective 1.2: environmental scan of what online services are being provided at other libraries (June of every year);
- Objective 1.3: establish online feedback survey (December 20xx);
- Objective 1.4: increase e-book holdings by 20 percent (December 2012);
- Objective 1.5: online resources retreat (June 2013).

Notice that each objective is numbered as a subset of the goal that it pertains to (1.1 = Goal 1's Objective 1) and that each has a specified ETA. Five objectives per goal is a maximum, otherwise both attention and resources become too diluted and unfocused. Here are the remaining Goals and Objectives.

Goal 2: comprehensive career resources and services

- Objective 2.1: review and revise currency of career resources and services (March 2012);
- Objective 2.2: provide career counseling workshops once a month (August 2011);
- Objective 2.3: expand online career resources by 30 percent (January 2012).

Goal 3: multi-faceted services and support for the homeless and indigent population

- Objective 3.1: targeted entertainment and technology resources and facilities (September 2011);
- Objective 3.2: quality information resources on housing, career training, substance abuse and other targeted support services (May 2011);
- Objective 3.3: market targeted services through appropriate venues (June 2011);
- Objective 3.4: conduct a social night once a month (July 2011).

Goal 4: world class youth and family collection and services

- Objective 4.1: increase collection budget by 20 percent (June 2012);
- Objective 4.2: mothers' social event once a month (March 2011);
- Objective 4.3: children's social event once a month (March 2011);
- Objective 4.4: technology and entertainment pantheon (March 2012).

Following such a strategic planning process compels organizations and their members to collaborate and create a shared vision of the present and future. It is absolutely critical, however, that the organization takes the time to determine what is important and what it wants to be particularly good at, and then allows all members a chance to contribute by helping to identify clear, objective ways in which to attain the stated goals. Strategic plans help both to unite the organization and to articulate the road map for where the organization is striving to be.

Customized fashion: finding the right fit

Abstract: Before planning for the future, we must understand the present and the past. This chapter takes an exhaustive look at current technology trends of public, academic, and school libraries. Networking, hardware, and software basics are covered in an easy-to-understand fashion designed for the layperson. Basic support questions librarians should expect to answer are also provided.

Key words: networking, hardware, software, technology infrastructure, computers, operating systems, local area network (LAN), bandwidth, user services, public, academic, school, Internet, technology FAQs.

The organization's goals have been articulated in a strategic plan that everyone has worked hard to create. Concrete objectives have been identified. Technology will invariably play a central role in helping establish both the infrastructure and the kinds of applications necessary to achieve a library's bottom line: access to information. Let us discuss some basic technology terms and tenets of robust, highly functional technology infrastructures.

Hardware and software

Technology hardware represents the physical material, the equipment, which represents the capacity for digital communications, interactions and processing to take place. It is typically more expensive than software and represents an organization's infrastructure to use and deliver technology solutions to both employees and users alike. Typical technology hardware includes cabling, computers, hand-held devices, tablets, monitors, scanners, wireless routers, barcodes, printers, flash drives, etc.

Technology software represents the digital computational code that both runs the hardware and runs on the hardware. So, for example, the cabling within an organization represents actual cables of wire (copper, fiber optic, etc.) that usually are located behind walls or in the ceiling, which are physically connected to a server within the building that is, in turn, connected physically to even larger cables run by an ISP. Software runs the router (a piece of hardware that 'routes' network traffic to the appropriate place) and computers that collectively comprise the *Internet* (computers 'interconnected' to one another through both cables and wireless radio waves) and the type and number of fibers within a cable serve as the capacity for digital data to move through them. Typical software we are most familiar with involves operating systems (Windows, Macintosh, Linux, etc.), browsers (Internet Explorer, Firefox, Chrome, etc.) and search engines and productivity software like Microsoft Office (Word, PowerPoint, Excel) and e-mail clients (i.e. Gmail, Hotmail, Outlook, Yahoo, etc.).

Let us first take a look at a typical hardware and software profile for a public library, academic library and school library and then go into a more specific discussion about common networking (wired and wireless protocol), hardware and software components.

A public library

The mid-sized public library interviewed for the book is located in the southeast United States and utilizes a three-year lease agreement for its computers that allows for: '... a standard established by the city technology department at the time of the lease. This allows predictable costs for computer equipment (for budgeting purposes) and guarantees that all computers are typically under warranty which streamlines the repair/replacement process.' Their network capacity is 20 Mbps (megabytes per second) and free wifi (wireless fidelity) at all library branches within the county. They have two separate networks, one for the public and one for staff, and the downtown library has a total of 123 computers, 108 of which are public computers connected to the Internet and have Microsoft Office. Ten of these computers are: 'reserved for catalog searches, two computers to run the microfilm readers and three Children's learning computers (these numbers vary a bit from year to year)' (Joseph, 2010).

The downtown public library has a self-checkout system and an automated system that checks in returned materials automatically. The public computers are run by a time-management system that limits sessions to one hour so that different users have a chance to use the computer. Printing is leased through a vending company that uses a vend-a-card system and every computer's connectivity to the Internet or bandwidth is managed using a filtering/shaping tool that manages overall network traffic.

Databases are subscribed to through a statewide consortium paid for collectively by all the state's public libraries. Access to this system allows for users to interact with a host of tools including 'professional journals and other periodicals, databases, testing materials, etc.', as well as e-books and other digital resources. As an institution, they also subscribe to 'Value Line, Tutor.com, Tumble-books, Rosetta Stone, Resume Maker, Newsbank (for the local paper), Netlibrary, Mango, Facts on File, Ellis, Dearreader.com, Antiques, Ancestry and a suite of children's learning software through a Gates grant'. They are also a subscriber to another statewide consortium that allows users 24/7 access to reference libraries online (ibid.).

The picture for the nation's public libraries shows a less promising picture – only 39 percent replaced their computers within four years or less while 42.4 percent had no computer replacement cycle at all. Wireless connectivity was not offered by 43.8 percent, and 77.7 percent reported that space limitations dictated how many computers they could make available to their patrons. In terms of IT support, 39 percent rely on IT support from untrained library staff, 38.5 percent rely on system level IT staff and 30 percent rely on outside vendors. In addition, demand is growing while funding and staffing remain static (Clark and Davis, 2009). In a recent study of 38 public libraries, librarians stated that, 'users now expect library services to resemble those in the marketplace . . . a 'MyLibrary.com' experience that allows for seamless integration across the library's services but also facilitates the use of personal technologies (e.g., iPods, MP3 players and USB devices)' (Bertot, 2009: 84).

In terms of online services, as would be expected, almost all US public libraries have a website (92.4 percent) (ALA, 2010). The library websites are usually managed by a librarian who manages it as part of his/her job

(50 percent), 'other' (either a volunteer or web committee; 18.4 percent), the IT department (13.3 percent), a dedicated non-librarian staff member (12.7 percent), more than one librarian (12.3 percent), an outside company (5.6 percent), or a librarian who does it as her/his sole job (2.8 percent) (Chow et al., 2011) (Figure 3.1).

Almost nine out of ten of the nation's public libraries do provide wireless connectivity to their patrons (88.2 percent) and almost half (46 percent) extend that access outside the library building so patrons can use the Internet around the building as well (ALA, 2010). Close to half of public libraries who responded to a nationwide survey provided some form of virtual reference services (49.3 percent). E-mail was the most often used by a large margin (83 percent), followed by chat (39.6 percent), or text messaging (19.4 percent) (Chow et al., 2011). In terms of managing bandwidth, most rural libraries (66 percent) in particular tend to have both wireless and dedicated wired Internet access on the same telecommunications connection which causes major traffic congestion and network slowdowns (ALA, 2010).

Social networking is also of increasing importance in public libraries. The major social networking tools currently used by US public libraries include Facebook (created in 2006), YouTube (created in 2005), Twitter (created in 2006), Flickr (created in 2004) and MySpace (created in 2003) (ibid.).

Facebook (*www.facebook.com*, Figure 3.2) is the most popular networking site in the world (over 500 million users worldwide) and its primary features include creating a personal or organizational profile and

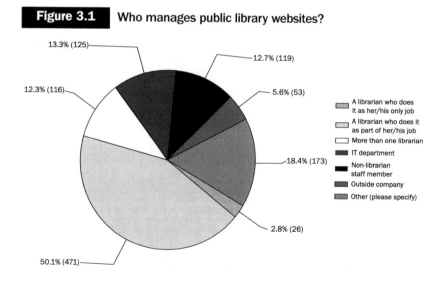

Figure 3.1 Who manages public library websites?

13.3% (125)
12.7% (119)
12.3% (116)
5.6% (53)
18.4% (173)
2.8% (26)
50.1% (471)

A librarian who does it as her/his only job
A librarian who does it as part of her/his job
More than one librarian
IT department
Non-librarian staff member
Outside company
Other (please specify)

Figure 3.2 Facebook

connecting with other profiles or accounts, which allows you to e-mail, blog, exchange photos and videos, and play games. Most importantly, through building connections with others by becoming 'friends' you can communicate quickly and easily completely free. Libraries primarily use Facebook so patrons can become friends with the library organization keeping them in touch with library events and announcements.

YouTube (*www.youtube.com*, Figure 3.3) is the world's largest free video repository allowing users to post up to 15 minutes or 2 GB of video (or unlimited for paid accounts) at a single time. This allows libraries to post and serve, via the Internet, promotional, instructional or documentary

Figure 3.3   YouTube

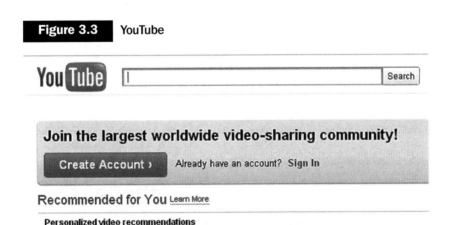

videos completely free. A library can create a dedicated YouTube channel that would allow them to serve and keep patrons aware of library events and activities.

Twitter (*www.twitter.com*, Figure 3.4) is an example of 'micro-blogging', or statements and reflections limited to 140 characters. These short statements are referred to as 'tweets' and they allow other people to follow your organization allowing quick communication through an electronic network.

Flickr (*www.flickr.com*, Figure 3.5) is one of the world's largest photo sharing sites (although it has been recently surpassed by Facebook). Libraries can create a free photo or video collection and generate professional slide shows to share images of library events and activities; many libraries, including the US Library of Congress, museums and archives use this service (ibid.).

MySpace (Figure 3.6) was the king of social marketing until 2007, but since then has dropped to fifth in overall users and changed its focus in 2009 to music and entertainment for the 13–24-year-old demographic (ibid.).

In 2009, close to 33 percent of all American adults used a social networking site at least once a month, which was twice the number of users in 2007 (ibid.).

Figure 3.4   Twitter

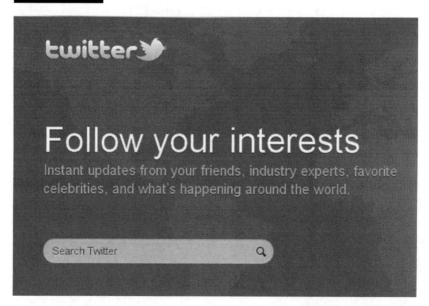

Figure 3.5 Flickr

Figure 3.6 MySpace

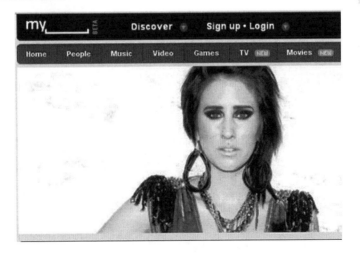

An academic library

An academic library at a public university also in the southeastern United States has 200 PC desktops, 50 laptops and 10 iPads as well as digital audio and video equipment available to the public for checkout, and an additional 135 desktops and laptops and 40 iPads for staff. All PCs are Windows machines and the various software applications are run by 12 Dell PowerEdge servers although some are running virtual servers (different server operating systems on the same machine). These servers are powering such services as the staff time clock, a production and test server (testing websites and other applications before rolling them live), two domain controllers (administrative computers that oversee all other servers), virus scans and imaging, hosting digital images and a web server. In addition, the library provides scanning and copier services, a teaching lab, multiple collaboratories (information commons), a touch-screen kiosk and self-check-out machines. All computers have standard Microsoft Office and security software.

Some locally-developed applications include Journal Finder, the first-ever developed OpenURL link resolver, a real time computer availability map, a resource scheduler, interactive tutorials and an information literacy game. Web 2.0 technologies include Blogger (Google blogs), Facebook (social networking), Flickr (photo sharing), Meebo (instant messaging) and Twitter (social networking).

Table 3.1 gives a snapshot of standard software on library computers.

Table 3.1 Academic library software

■ Acrobat	■ Illustrator
■ Acrobat Reader	■ Internet Explorer
■ Ariel	■ IRAS
■ Audacity	■ Jaws
■ Connexion	■ LC Easy
■ Contribute	■ Lotus Notes
■ DeskTracker	■ Microsoft Office
■ DivX	■ NetChk*
■ Dreamweaver	■ Odyssey
■ Eraser	■ OmniPage
■ Firefox	■ Password Safe
■ Iliad	■ Perfect Disk

■ Photoshop	■ Symantec AntiVirus
■ Photoshop Elements	■ TimeClock
■ PowerDVD	■ Visual Studio
■ QuickTime	■ Windows Live Messenger
■ Realplayer	■ Workflows
■ Roxio Creator	■ ZoomText
■ SQL Server	

Source: Bucknall, 2010.

A report from Academic Colleges and Research Libraries suggests that 'changes in higher education will require that librarians possess diverse skill sets', and that 'demands for accountability and assessment will increase' (ACRL Research Planning and Review Committee, 2010: 287). Libraries will need to move with the needs of their academic constituencies (i.e. administration, faculty and students) as they leverage emerging technologies, and accountability to those institutions they serve will play an increasingly important role in justifying their existence as universities reorganize themselves to meet the changing needs of the 21st century. Furthermore, in terms of technology trends the report concludes:

> Cloud computing, augmented and virtual reality, discovery tools, open content, open source software and new social networking tools are some of the most important technological changes affecting academic libraries. As with mobile applications, these developments will affect nearly all library operations. (ibid.: 289)

For academic libraries, in terms of maintaining their websites, similarly to public libraries, the overwhelming majority (51 percent) have a librarian who does it as part of her/his job. The IT department is a distant second at 19.1 percent followed by 'Other' (librarian and other team, a web committee, etc.) at 17.9 percent, more than one librarian (15.7 percent), a non-librarian staff member (13.8 percent), a librarian who does it solely as her/his job (4.4 percent) and an outside company (2.8 percent) (Figure 3.7).

In terms of reference services, the results of a large-scale study at The University of North Carolina at Greensboro showed that 69 percent of randomly selected student respondents had used some form of reference services (Figure 3.8). While face-to-face reference (55.6 percent) was substantially more popular than all types of virtual reference, students used online chat (27.8 percent) most frequently, followed by e-mail (22.4 percent), telephone (11.2 percent) and text (2.7 percent), which was surprisingly low (Chow and Croxton, 2011).

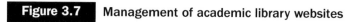

Figure 3.7 Management of academic library websites

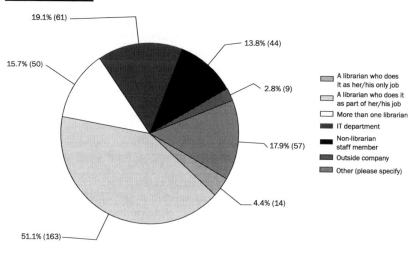

19.1% (61)
13.8% (44)
15.7% (50)
2.8% (9)
17.9% (57)
4.4% (14)
51.1% (163)

A librarian who does it as her/his only job
A librarian who does it as part of her/his job
More than one librarian
IT department
Non-librarian staff member
Outside company
Other (please specify)

Figure 3.8 Student reference service preferences

Which of the following library reference services have you used at the UNCG University Libraries? (Check all that apply.)

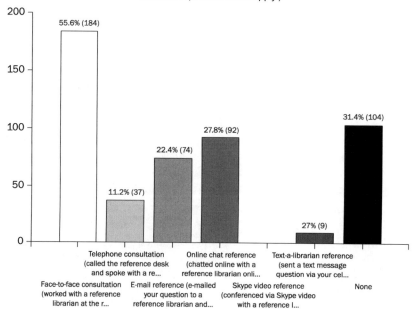

200

55.6% (184)

150

100

31.4% (104)

27.8% (92)

50

22.4% (74)

11.2% (37)

27% (9)

0

Telephone consultation (called the reference desk and spoke with a re...
Online chat reference (chatted online with a reference librarian onli...
Text-a-librarian reference (sent a text message question via your cel...

Face-to-face consultation (worked with a reference librarian at the r...
E-mail reference (e-mailed your question to a reference librarian and...
Skype video reference (conferenced via Skype video with a reference l...
None

For quick facts, students preferred the brevity of a quick telephone call, followed by an online chat session, e-mail and then text (Figure 3.9).

For more complicated research questions, however, students preferred e-mail first, online chat second and telephone third, with Skype video and texting a distant fourth and fifth, respectively (Figure 3.10).

As you might surmise, faculty, however, had different preferences (Figure 3.11). Sixty-six percent had used some form of reference service with face-to-face still being the preferred method at 53 percent. Unlike students, however, the most preferred virtual reference service for faculty and staff was e-mail (39.9 percent) followed by telephone (29.4 percent). Only 13.9 percent preferred online chat which was the most popular virtual reference type for students.

For help answering a quick fact, telephone was the first choice of faculty and staff, followed by e-mail, online chat, text and Skype video (Figure 3.12).

For a longer research question, however, as with students, faculty and staff preferred e-mail overall, telephone and online chat as well as text and Skype video (Figure 3.13).

Figure 3.9   Student virtual reference preferences (quick facts)

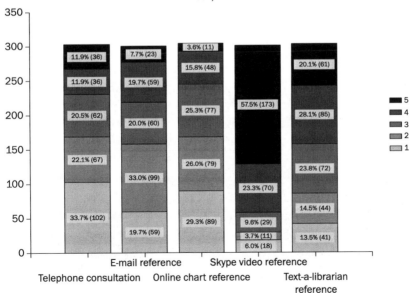

Please rank order your preference of virtual reference formats (1 = highest, 5 = lowest) if you needed help finding a quick fact (example: finding the hours of the library for the week)

Figure 3.10

Figure 3.10 — Student virtual reference preferences (for a research question)

Please rank order your preference of virtual reference formats (1 = highest, 5 = lowest) if you needed help locating materials for a research project (example: locating biographical information for an author without using Google)

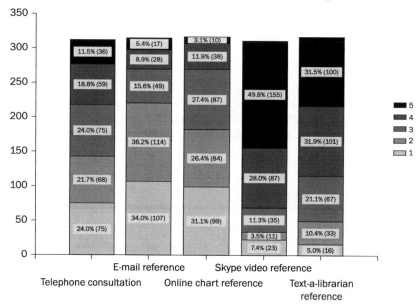

Figure 3.11 — Faculty and staff reference preferences

Which of the following library reference services have you used at the UNCG University Libraries? (Check all that apply.)

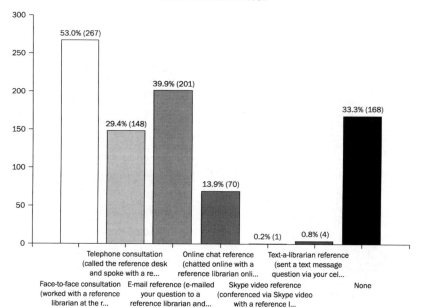

Figure 3.12

Faculty and staff virtual reference preferences (quick facts)

Please rank order your preference of virtual reference formats (1 = highest, 5 = lowest) if you needed help finding a quick fact (example: finding the hours of the library for the week)

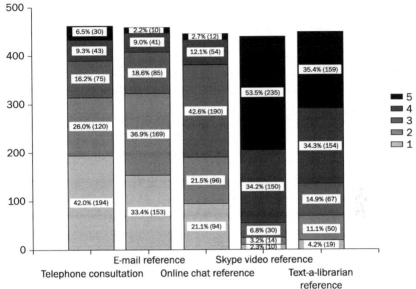

Figure 3.13

Faculty and staff virtual reference preferences (for a research question)

Please rank order your preference of virtual reference formats (1 = highest, 5 = lowest) if you needed help locating materials for a research project (example: locating biographical information for an author without using Google)

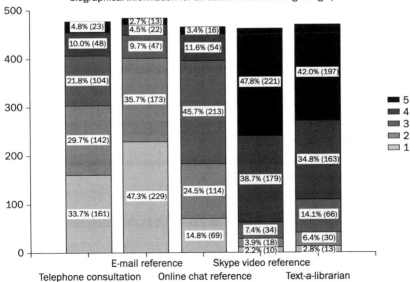

A school library

A mid-sized school district in the southeastern United States was asked to describe the hardware and software environment of a typical school in its district. Each school has 20–50 MB connectivity to the desktop and 250 MB connectivity to the district's Internet backbone provided by its ISP. In preparation for an increase in usage of streaming media, bandwidth shaping (which limits or provides more bandwidth based on current need) is used with multi-broadcast access. The school library is wireless using an 80211n standard, and battery outlets are strategically placed throughout the building. This standard allows for VoIP or voice/video over the Internet. A cable channel feed digitizer (digitizes cable feed so it can be streamed on LCD projectors) is used so teachers can more easily display cable feeds to an entire class.

Laptops are available for checkout, as are handheld devices such as tablet PCs, iPads or iPod Touches. They also have charging stations for various mobile devices. Multifunctional copier/scanner/printers are used, which allows for maximum flexibility and efficiency of use and space. Self-service checkout stations are available. Also for checkout are flip video cameras, webcams and headsets to be used for meetings and presenting over the Internet. The library also houses a multimedia production editing area with high-end video and production equipment.

In terms of software, outside the standard Microsoft Office and other application software, Adobe Creative Suite or iMovie are used for editing and compiling video and audio files. For video collaboration the district uses Elluminate, Wimba and WebEx. They also use an electronic courseware credit recovery software application that is used by students who may have fallen behind that allows them to catch up in an independent, self-paced fashion. Databases include online access to the library collection, e-books, a consortium for peer-reviewed texts, digital histories related to the school (e.g. yearbooks, local newspapers, etc.), Discovery education and other k12 video streaming services and PD360 or other similar professional development best practices videos (Frye, 2010).

Nationwide technology trends school librarians should be aware of include the increase of teachers leveraging existing student mobile devices for delivering mobile content in the classroom without having to provide 1:1 device to student coverage, an increase in web-based instruction and the use of interactive, real-time assessment that complements 'clicker' technology allowing teachers the opportunity to determine if students truly 'get it' (McCrea, 2010). In addition, cloud computing (which allows multiple users to share limited licenses across a network) will proliferate as its use will realize significant savings by not having to license software on a 1:1 machine-to-license basis along with the need for teacher professional development necessary to provide teachers with the training to be able to use this emerging technology (McCrea, 2010).

It is clear that social media also plays a significant role for students in schools, and school libraries should try and support this use as one of its primary services; according to Danah Boyd, online social media expert in school libraries, 'In the same way that you keep the doors open in schools, you need to keep the digital doors open on line' (ALA, 2010: 26).

Library technology infrastructures and user services

President Obama believes that all Americans should have access to broadband and the transformative opportunities it affords. Broadband services allow individuals to access new career and educational opportunities. They help businesses reach new markets and improve efficiency. They support struggling communities that seek to attract new industries. And they enhance the government's capacity to deliver critical services. (US Department of Commerce National Telecommunications and Information Administration, 2010: 1)

Networking, hardware and software are the three major components of technology infrastructure. From a user standpoint the network is experienced, for the most part, by how fast they are able to access applications and resources on the Internet (e.g. web surfing, sending e-mails, downloading documents, etc.). According to a US Department of Commerce report (2010) over 30 percent of Americans do not use the Internet nor do they have access to the Internet at home. Of those that do have access to the Internet at home, 35 percent do not have broadband with the most common reasons being 'lack of need' or 'too expensive'.

As would be expected, over a 12-year period from 1997 to 2009, computer and Internet use increased significantly (Figure 3.14). Households with computers increased from 36.6 percent to 61.8 percent, while Internet access at home increased from only 18.6 percent in 1997 to 68.7 percent in 2009. Access to broadband, defined as any connection faster than a dial-up connection (e.g. DSL, Cable, wireless), also exploded during this time from 4.4 percent in 2000 to 63.5 percent in 2009.

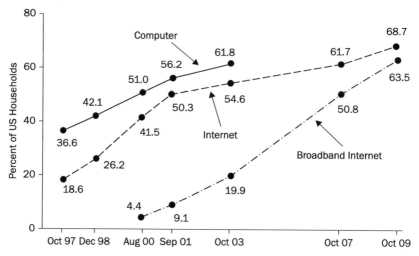

Figure 3.14 Computer and Internet growth in the US, 1997–2009

Source: *Digital Nation.* National Telecommunications and Information Administration, US Department of Commerce, 2010.
Note: 2001, 2003, 2007 and 2009 Census-based weights and earlier years use 1990 Census-based weights.

Access to broadband was positively attributed to employment status, living in an urban vs. rural area and household family income (Figure 3.15 and Figure 3.16).

Networking basics

Let us begin our discussion of technology by dissecting each of the main parts individually. We will start with networking. A network is simply a group of two or more computers connected together – either through cable, wirelessly, or through a combination of both. Within the context of the library examples above, networking represents the connection each computer has to a local area network (LAN) or a group of connected computers. The common elements of a network are as shown in Table 3.2.

Let us walk step-by-step through how everything is connected to one another starting from the computer and work our way up to how they are connected to the Internet.

Figure 3.15 Broadband home access by employed and urban status, 2007–2009

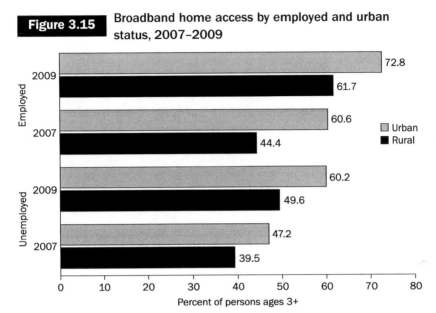

Source: Digital Nation. National Telecommunications and Information Administration, US Department of Commerce, 2010.

Figure 3.16 Access to broadband by income, 2007–2009

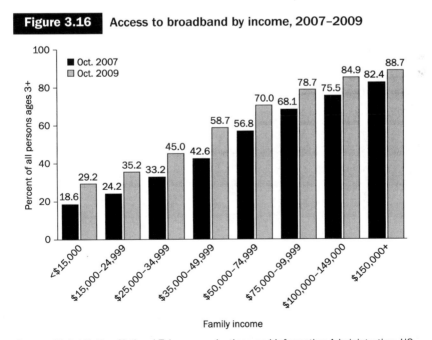

Source: Digital Nation. National Telecommunications and Information Administration, US Department of Commerce, 2010.

Table 3.2   Networking basics

Networking term	Description
Node	Anything that is connected to your network – usually printers and computers.
Segment	These are the 'areas' of your network that are separated from each other and connected by a switch, router, etc. (e.g. staff computers in an office and a computer lab represent two different segments in a network).
Backbone	This is the main cabling that all segments are connected to and is usually much faster. Staff computers, for example, are physically connected to the network by cables in the wall. The cable connected to that one computer requires less capacity than the main cable that includes all simultaneous computer data from all staff computers in that area.
Topology	Networks can be arranged in many different ways. The particular configuration in which the computers are connected to one another is called its 'topology'. Bus, Ring, Star and Mesh topologies are some of the most popular and efficient network configurations.
Local Area Network (LAN) and Wide Area Network (WAN)	Computers in one building that are connected to each other form a 'Local' area network (LAN). Computers that are connected to each other (different LANS in other words) that are in different buildings or beyond (i.e. at a school or university) form a 'Wide' area network (WAN)
Network Interface Card (NIC card) and/ or wireless interface (WIC card)	This is your computer's 'network card' that allows it to communicate with your local area network. It is what the network cable plugs into in the back of your computer. Almost all laptops, smartphones, PDAs, tablets, etc. also have a wireless interface card (WIC) that allows them to connect to a wireless network.
WiFi or Wireless Fidelity	This is the term used for IEEE standard 802.11, which defines how manufacturers should engineer wireless devices and capacity. The substandards for WiFi are 802.11a (54 Mbps or Megabits per second) and 802.11b (11 Mbps) in 1999, 802.11g (54 Mbps) in 2002 which had greater range and 802.11n (100 Mbps) in 2009. Bluetooth (1–3 Mbps) is the popular standard for handheld devices (IEEE, 2011; About.com, 2011).
Media Access Control (MAC) Address	Like an ID card, this is your computer's ID card to access the network. More specifically, each MAC address is exactly six digits – three digits for the manufacturer and three digits that are the unique three digit identifier every NIC has. Collectively, this number allows a specific computer access to a local area network.

The need for speed, well paved roads and traffic cops

Each computer, which is called a node or connection point on the network, will be connected to any other computer through cables connected to it, most likely using an Ethernet connection (or port) usually in the wall. The term 'Ethernet' is another networking standard that means simply *all computers will be connected to each other using the same communication line of cables* and is derived from the basic principle established by standard 802.3 of the Institute of Electrical and Electronics Engineers (IEEE, 2008). The speed of a network, or the amount of information that can be passed through the cables at one time, is defined by the size and types of the wires housed within the cable that form your network.

———	'Thin' wire is the slowest as it can only pass through 'small' amounts of information.
———	'Thick' wire is faster as more information can pass through it at one time.
▬▬▬	'Twisted' pair of usually copper-based wires increase the amount of pass-through of information, which allows for 10 Mbps (Megabites per second)
———	Thousands of fiber optic wires that transmit light through thin pieces of glass, which allows up to 100 Mbps. Communication through light works similar to Morris code where light signals are used to send and decode messages (computers do this automatically of course).
═══	Double 'Twisted' pairs of usually copper-based wires, referred to as CAT 5 cabling or Category 5 cabling which allows for 1000 Mbps or 1 Gbps (Gigabites per second)
═══	Thousands of fiber optic wires operating through wider multi-mode fiber optic wires, which allows for up to 10 Gbps of information processing speed.

This cable connects the computer to the LAN's backbone, which is usually a more robust cable that allows transmission of data from multiple computers and other nodes (i.e. printers, servers, wireless routers, etc.) at the same time. There are actually four primary network configurations: Bus, Ring, Star and Mesh topologies.

- *Bus topology:* All computers are connected directly to the network's backbone similar to a fishbone.

- *Ring topology:* All computers are connected to the backbone and to each other in a closed circuit where each must take its turn sending and receiving data.

- *Star topology:* All computers are connected to a hub or switch that is then connected to the backbone.

- *Mesh topology:* All computers are connected to each other and also to the backbone. A partial mesh topology is one of the more popular ones today as it allows redundancy or alternate pathways for essential services just in case something fails.

There are three primary types of hardware that help connect segments of computers or devices to one another and the backbone: *hubs, switches* and *routers* (Tyson, 2001).

- A *hub* is simply a connection point between computers. It does not filter or direct traffic in any fashion.

- *Switches,* on the other hand, serve as the traffic cops of the network that direct traffic to where it wants and needs to go by recognizing patterns in traffic and sending information directly to the right part of the network. This allows for more efficient and quicker networks.

- *Routers* direct the same traffic that *switches* do but in more advanced ways and with more customizability – in essence they 'understand' and recognize data traffic and can prioritize which type of data moves faster, limit how much network bandwidth types of data can take, and actually shape bandwidth usage in real-time so that there are few network slowdowns (e.g. one computer needs more bandwidth and the router will give that computer and its data traffic priority over other traffic so there are no slowdowns in data transfer).

The time it takes for data to transfer and reach its destination is called its *latency.*

Wireless access points and routers

Wireless access points are in fact radio transmitters and represent a node, just like a computer, on a local area network (LAN). The 802.11 standard designates the radio frequencies used and wireless access points (WAPs) serve as the connection point for both sending out and receiving wireless radio signals that then are physically joined to an organization's LAN. The type of wireless interface cards (b, g, or n) that these transmitters contain will determine how much and how far the wireless network extends or broadcasts. Whether the wireless access point serves also as a router just depends on which type of WAP is used. Devices that have wireless interface cards will be able to interface with available wireless networks in range; cell phone carriers, also using radio waves although at different frequencies (824–94 MHz) than the 802.11 standard (2.4 GHz or 5 GHz) (Horton, 2008), can also deliver access to Internet services either through phones, laptops, etc.

Servers

One of the final pieces of the network central nervous system is a server, which is a computer that has the capacity to process and house a lot more information than a regular desktop computer. These specialized computers run specific applications that help provide services or applications to all other computers on the network, such as network security and authentication, e-mail, network space, printing, backup and storage and, most importantly, web services (e.g. where your organization's website lives, web-based applications). In the end, though, servers are nothing more than higher-capacity computers that have a specific function or purpose. Later on we will discuss the growing popularity of virtualization, which more efficiently uses the hardware capacity of one server to run many different applications at the same time.

The Internet truly makes the world go round

For many library users, the most important connection in a network is its connection to the Internet. Without that, users could only e-mail other people within the library and access only the library's web pages. But what exactly is the Internet? Who controls the Internet and how much of 'it' does an organization actually get? Let us walk through this step-by-step. From a topology standpoint, the bandwidth an organization has to the Internet is determined by its cabling and the amount of bandwidth it has leased from an ISP. Let us take a moment to discuss what exactly the Internet is, who runs it and how we gain access to it.

The Internet is by definition a connection of computers and other nodes or devices. It is governed by the same rules we have discussed but at much larger capacity – much bigger cables, much bigger routers and much bigger and faster bandwidth. In essence no one really owns or controls the Internet as nodes to it are controlled by anyone who wants to pay to access it. When you buy Internet service from your local ISP and connect a computer to it, then you have added another node to the Internet itself. With that being said, there are a finite number of mega multi-national companies like IBM, Sprint, AT&T and Verizon that provide the cabling, routers and people power to keep the Internet up and running and they compete with each other and also represent multiple-points of failure, so if one goes down the Internet lives on through the others. These are referred to as upstream ISPs who then charge thousands of smaller ISPs for access, and these in turn ultimately charge businesses and individuals (Strickland, 2008). Governments and companies alike have to pay to access the Internet.

Remember that providing physical cabling across the world means literally providing cables across oceans, deserts, etc. and the cost of design, development and maintenance is enormous and ongoing. The upstream ISPs charge the smaller ISPs a monthly fee and they in turn charge the consumer a monthly fee. How much your organization pays an ISP will determine how much access to the Internet backbone it is allowed to have.

Networking profiles of our case studies

Both the public and school libraries in our case study use bandwidth shaping, which provides more bandwidth to users, or limits bandwidth usage, based on whether or not a given task requires it (e.g. video or music streaming). This minimizes the likelihood of slow downloads thereby reducing user frustration. Network speed is controlled primarily by the amount of bandwidth purchased through the organization's ISP, by the type of cabling that connects the organization to the ISP and also by the individual computer's connections to the organization's servers. The academic library, with more resources, has 1 Gbps to the desktop through fiber optic cabling and a larger bandwidth agreement with its ISP. The public and school libraries have 20–50 Mbps to the desktop, considerably slower, but still more than sufficient to support the needs of its users (public and employees). All three have free wireless services, which have become an expectation for library users as ownership of laptops and other wireless devices (i.e. smart phones, iPods, tablets, etc.) has risen.

Networking support FAQs

1. How can I tell if it is the computer, browser, network or ISP that is having connectivity problems?

When a computer cannot connect there are many things to try to determine where exactly the problem lies. First is to open another browser as the browser may have just frozen. Another quick option is to check another website to make sure the problem does not rest specifically with the website that the user is trying to access. Certainly another option is to check another computer within that network segment as a network outage would mean all computers would be cut off from the network. Also, always check the cables at the back of the computer. Lastly, for Windows machines, you can use the 'cmd' and 'ping' [insert website address] option to 'ping' the server of a website you are trying to access to ensure that website's server is receiving and sending out packets of information. Just go to Start and then type in *cmd*.

2. *How do I determine a computer's IP address?*

Again, for Windows machines type in 'cmd' to get to your computer's command prompt and then enter in 'ipconfig' to see your computer's IP address and to make sure it is active and able to send and receive network information.

3. *What is an IP address and how is it related to a web address?*

Internet Protocol (IP) is based on four sets of numbers called octets (each of the four sets of numbers can actually have eight distinct numbers). So if you ping *www.google.com*, you will find their IP address to be: 74.125.47.106. The first octet, 74, designates Google's network ID while the remaining three octets identify the specific host and node identification of the web server hosting Google's website. Web addresses simply add a text descriptor and organizer to otherwise intimidating and hard to remember numerical IP addresses.

Hardware basics

Now that we have a basic understanding of how networking works let us take a look at some of the major hardware that uses it: computers, mobile devices, e-readers, RFID technology and self-checkout automation. Like the networking section, this covers some of the basic hardware that staff may be exposed to and are expected to support in a library and information organization.

Computing basics

According to Webster's Dictionary a computer is 'a programmable usually electronic device that can store, retrieve and process data' (*Merriam-Webster Dictionary*, n.d.(b)). The word computer can be traced to the Latin words *Putare* that means 'to determine by mathematical means' and *com* which is a prefix that adds emphasis. In layman's terms within the context of our discussion a computer simply is a hardware device that is able to compute, store, display and retrieve digital data.

Let us start with the actual piece of hardware that does the computing: the data micro-processing chip or, as more commonly known, the central processing unit (CPU). The key component of this chip is the number of micro transistors on the same integrated circuit that actually powers the data crunching or processing. The first chip was created in 1974 and contained 6,000 transistors and had a clock speed, the amount of data cycles that can be processed per second per million (megahertz), of 2 MHz. Intel co-founder Gordon Moore is credited with the famous Moore's Law, which states that the number of transistors that can be placed on the same integrated circuit will double every two years. In 2004, the top clock speed was a Pentium chip (made by Intel) at 3.5 GHz, data cycles that can be processed per second per billion. In 2011, while IBM has developed a mainframe computer with a CPU clock speed of 5.2 GHz, commercially the top-end clock speed remained at 3.5 GHz. Worldwide, there are currently two main manufacturers of the micro-processing chip: Intel and AMD. Apple used to also create their own PowerPC microprocessors but discontinued them in 2006 in favor of Intel. Clock speed has remained relatively static due to current engineering limitations on the number of micro transistors that can be etched on an integrated circuit as well as management of the amount of heat produced by complex mathematical calculations.

While these micro-processing units or CPUs are considered the 'brains' of a computer, motherboards (circuit boards that house and manage the transactions of all a computer's components) are considered the computer's central nervous system. The motherboard connects the two other main components of a computer – storage (hard disc drive) and retrieval (Random Access Memory). Hard drives are the main storage device of a computer that houses most software applications (i.e. the operating system, production software, files, etc.) and are usually the size of a regular paperback novel. Additional external hard drives can be purchased at relatively low cost to supplement hard drive space if needed. Hard drive space is measured in terms of Megabytes (MB or 1,000 kilobytes of data),

Gigabytes (GB or 1,000 MB of data) and now Terrabytes (TB or 1,000 GB of data) of digital storage space. Hard drives are a set of spinning discs that have data imprinted on them through electromagnetic images or patterns of thin layers of glass or metal alloy that can be written and read by micro-processing units. Hard drives are typically stored as a drive near the front of a computer directly under or over the CD/DVD drive.

Random Access Memory (RAM) is one of a suite of types of memory a computer needs to run effectively. How much RAM a computer has dictates how many simultaneous software applications can be run at one time. The more you have the more you are able to do (applications opened and working simultaneously) without experiencing a computer slow down (your computer cannot effectively process all of the process calculations requested). Other devices connected to the motherboard that are essential for a computer's functioning include a graphics card, a sound card, power supply, fan for dissipating the heat produced by your CPUs, monitor, mouse and keyboard.

Mobile devices

Cell phones

According to a 2009 United Nations report, over half of the world's population now has a cell phone (Beaumont, 2009) with an increase of 300 percent from 1 billion users in 2002 to 4.1 billion users in 2009. In the United States, as of December 2010, an estimated 96 percent of Americans (302 million) have access to wireless of some kind – a 45 percent increase from 2005 (CTIA, 2010). The US also has more unique 3G (voice and data wireless) wireless subscribers, 123.2 million, than the five largest European Union countries combined (France, Germany, Italy, Spain and UK).

The term 3G stands for 'third generation' cell phone network standards, which simply allows cell phones and other mobile devices to transfer data more quickly to accommodate multi-media recordings, images and data sharing more effectively. 3G phones are referred to as the first generation 'smart phones'. 1G or first generation phones were analog voice, and 2G or second generation cell phones allowed for roaming and initial data transfer beyond voice. There is also a 4G iPhone from Apple.

PDAs, Pocket PCs and Smart Phones

Personal digital assistants (PDAs) and pocket personal computers (Pocket PCs) are portable devices that really have three primary functions:

personal information management services (PIMS), running application and production software and synchronizing with a personal computer (Freudenrich and Carmack, n.d.). Pocket PCs are for the most part just PDAs that run the Windows mobile operating system and Smart Phones are PDAs that have telephone service and capability.

Tablet PCs

Although tablet PCs existed before the iPad, it was this device that has launched the tablet PC phenomenon, with a form factor much lighter and portable than a laptop and a much wider screen than a PDA. Interestingly enough, because these tablets are for the most part not using either Windows or Intel technology, they represent a truly new age to the computing industry not ruled by Microsoft or Intel. Following the success of the iPad, major competitors are rolling out their own tablet PCs and collectively they are projected to represent approximately up to 33 percent of all PC purchases by as early as 2012 (McDougall, 2010). While content creation remains the realm of a laptop or desktop, 'content consumers' seem to prefer the lighter, smaller tablet PC for file and music sharing and accessing e-mails and other information (Sperling, 2010).

Digital e-readers

Similar to mobile technology, e-readers have been around for many years. It was the advent of the E Ink technology developed out of MIT Media labs that was then adopted by Sony as their e-reader standard that spawned today's digital readers because of its 'low power consumption and high contrast, combined with the fact that it is a reflective, rather than transmissive, display, so it is easier on the eyes while using less power' (Griffey, 2010: 7). Primary e-readers on the market as of 2011 include: Amazon's Kindle, Barnes & Nobles' Nook, Sony's Reader, Apple's iPad, Bookeen's Cybook, iREX's iLiad (Larson, 2010). All current e-readers can now read the standard PDF format typically associated with a standardized digital e-book file, and text-to-voice capabilities are now commonly available so that the digital e-book can be read out loud.

Radio Frequency Identification (RFID) tags

RFID tags are tags with a tiny microchip which stores information about the item to which it is attached. In addition, it has a radio antenna that receives and transfers information from and to an RFID reader. They were first used to track cattle in the late 1970s but now are inexpensive enough to be used in mass quantities for items such as books. While they cost anywhere from 7–12 cents, RFID tags are growing in popularity with libraries as they enable them to manage their collections more efficiently and effectively.

Self check-out, self service and automated fine payments

Bottom line: the more users can do for themselves, the more library staff can utilize limited resources to do other things. While seen as a threat by some, a *Library Journal* study (Dempsey, 2010) of the nation's public libraries (n = 834) found that both staff and patrons were highly satisfied with self service and self check-out options because they freed staff to do other things (72 percent) and eased congestion (67 percent), which has led to much quicker turnaround in terms of getting returned books back into circulation. Dempsey's study found that the average start-up cost for a self check-out system was from $20,000 and up to $1.2 million for the largest library systems. Self check-out machines typically involve users checking out library resources by scanning their library cards and then scanning the specific library resources' barcodes. Utilizing RDIF tags allows for the process to occur as a group by placing the items on the check-out device allowing for it to automatically scan all items at the same time.

Automated fine payment systems have also been identified by public libraries as a wave of the future. It is predicted that as high as 60 percent will adopt some method of automated online payment system by 2012, as this allows for 'significant decreases in the number of customers with "stops" because of excessive fines, fewer errors from staff handling cash and, perhaps most important in an age of budget cuts, increased revenue from customers' expanded opportunities to make payments' (Dempsey, 2010: 25).

Hardware support FAQs:

1. Is it cheaper to buy or make your own computers?

   In the hands of someone with experience, it would appear to be cheaper in the short-term to build your own computers. Beyond this initial short-term lower cost in terms of parts only,

---

however, building your own computers will cost more in terms of parts (limited warranties on each part), time spent building them and overall loss of person power for the building and maintaining of them. Buying computers with a full three-year warranty is the most cost effective and is a better allocation of people resources in the mid and long term.

2. *Should we keep computers that are no longer under warranty?*

Buying new computers is expensive and it may very well be a financial necessity to keep computers that are working just fine under the 'if it ain't broke, don't fix it' line of thinking. With that being said, using computers that never were under warranty or have run out of their warranty, places the organization squarely in a reactive mode of being. In other words, it is a given that a computer will eventually fail and waiting for it to do so introduces chaos, unhappy users, unexpected costs and, in general, a loss of productivity and general frustration and anxiety, the collective cost of which is immeasurable. Recommended replacement cycles include 25 percent or 33 percent of older computers every year or replacing all of them at the end of every three years (when the warranty runs out).

3. *Help! A patron is asking me to help them with a computer that is frozen. What should I do?*

This is usually a software issue (your operating system has frozen) rather than a hardware issue. For Windows, the usual solution is pressing the CTRL + ALT + DELETE buttons which will allow you to terminate manually any applications that are running. For Macs it is usually a CTRL + right click of the mouse that will allow you to close the frozen application. When all else fails, reboot the computer by pushing and holding the power down for five seconds.

4. *A computer will not turn on, what should I do?*

There are a whole host of steps to try and determine what is wrong. First and foremost, is making sure there is power. Is the power cord plugged into the back of the computer and also into the wall? If so, are you sure that the power outlet is working (plug something else in if possible)? Also check the monitor for the same issues. Take a look to see if the computer's power light is on – either in the front and/or back of the computer. Next, determine whether in fact the computer is not working or it is the operating system – is the computer showing any indications of being on or is the hard drive or CPUs doing any work at all? Rebooting the computer is always something to try as well. If none of the above works then the computer will need to be looked at by an IT technician.

5. *My older computers are running fine but appear to just be unable to handle the new software installed on them. Do I need to replace them?*

Under the big assumption that your computer is virus, spyware and malware free and there are no problems with the operating systems, then it may very well be that the new software is designed for larger capacity RAM and processing speed (as well as graphics) then an older computer may be able to handle. Software developers usually try and take advantage of the newest hardware capabilities, and using hardware technology that is more than four years old usually results in significant slowdowns.

6. *Should we buy PCs or Macintosh computers?*

Most IT directors will immediately answer PCs over Macs for a variety of reasons – per computer cost (differences of more than a few dollars per item over many items is significant), knowledge and familiarity of employees and users to a Windows operating system, interoperability of software (most software is built for Windows) and in general a lesser 'hassle' factor that is also a critical competent of overall smooth functioning in an already high-stress, high-anxiety environment. This has nothing to do with the overall 'quality' of a computer per se but is rather a question of overall efficiency and cost.

Because of the amazingly complex degree of engineering and the number of different parts involved in making a computer work, there are numerous points of failure that can cause a computer to stop working. As noted above, this is also why it is a good idea to replace your computers after their warranties have expired – failure of one of these components is inevitable and, if they continue to work, they may not be robust enough to run the new software, which is based on newer hardware, quickly enough to avoid significant slowdowns and user/employee frustration.

Hardware profiles of our case studies

Hardware profiles are consistent across the three types of libraries. Windows desktop computers are predominant for both the public and employees, with Microsoft Office along with a basic suite of software. The public library uses a lease agreement that ensures their computing is upgraded every three years and remains under warranty, which also enables them to plan for consistent expenditures and ensure all computers are in good shape. These machines are for individual use and some are dedicated for catalog searches and microfilm reading. All three libraries have laptops, video/audio agreement and handheld devices for checkout for both the public and staff; and all three also have self check-out machines and printing/copying/scanning services. As one might expect, the academic library, while offering similar services, simply has more of everything because of its larger, more technology proficient user base – a larger infrastructure in general with more servers, more computers, more laptops and more handheld devices for checkout. This also comes with a larger IT staff – five full-time staff for the academic in comparison to two for the public library and one for the school library.

Software basics

In this section we discuss software basics, including the major categories, how it runs and interacts with computer hardware and how it is displayed on computer monitors.

Bits and Bytes

It really is all about 0s and 1s. A BIT is actually short for Binary DigIT, which operates using only the two digits 0 and 1. Eight Bits (can be eight 0s, eight 1s, or any combination thereof (256 to be exact)) equals one Byte of information. One character of information is equivalent to one Byte of information. This is the basis for measuring connection speeds (i.e. Mbps or Mega*bits* per second) and storage (i.e. MB is Mega*byte*) (Table 3.3).

Word processing documents that only use text are relatively small – typically around 50 to 100 KB in size. Once you start adding images and figures, that number will jump above 100 KB and up into the MB size. The size of image files is primarily dependent on their resolution (or quality). The more pixels, the larger the file size. As you might expect, video (1–100 MB or larger) and sound files can be quite large, with sizes ranging from 10–100 MB.

Table 3.3 Connection speeds and storage

Connection speeds		Storage	
Speed in Bits per second	Type of connection	Storage capacity for hard drives and RAM	Total Bytes
10 Mbps (Megabits Per Second)	802.11 wireless (Bluetooth is 1–3 Mbps)	1 KB (Kilobyte)	1,024 Bytes
100 Mbps	802.11n wireless (802.11a and 802.11g is up to 54 Mbps); fiber optic cabling	1 MB (Megabyte)	1,048,576 Bytes
1 Gbps	CAT5 cabling, fiber optic cabling	1 GB (Gigabyte)	1,073,741,824 Bytes
10 Gbps +	Large fiber optic cables that comprise Internet backbones	1 TB (Terrabyte)	1 trillion Bytes or 1,000 GB

Operating systems

The world's first computers did not have operating systems. Instead they merely crunched data they were given to process. In order to perform computations, programmers and scientists had to write the instructions, place them on punch cards or tapes and then manually insert them into the computer. Imagine a line of scientists and researchers standing in the hallway awaiting their turn to access a computer that would crunch their data for them. Soon these single sets of commands became bunched into a series of commands, which became the precursor to the first computer operating systems (*History of Operating Systems*, n.d.).

A computer operating system is defined as 'software that controls the operation of a computer and directs the processing of programs (as by assigning storage space in memory and controlling input and output systems) (*Merriam-Webster Online Dictionary*, n.d.(c)). Its purpose '. . . is to organize and control hardware and software so that the device it lives in behaves in a flexible but predictable way' (Franklin and Coustan, 2000). There are three primary computer operating systems – Microsoft Windows, Apple Macintosh OS and UNIX (or Linux which is a UNIX derivative). The emergence of Tablet computers has also introduced some new mobile operating systems although Windows' and Apple's mobile operating systems still dominate the market.

Functionally, operating systems really have two primary functions – managing the hardware and software resources of your computer (how they communicate and interact with one another), and providing a standardized way for software applications to interact with your computer's hardware (which varies by make, model and manufacturer) (ibid.). Similar to the first computers, your computer's processors need to know what to compute and then where to send the end results (for example, your graphics card is a piece of hardware that sends output to your monitor). Without the operating system your computer will not be able to function.

Network operating systems – security, authentication and sharing resources

Unfortunately, computer hacking has existed almost as long as computers themselves. But with early computers, you had to be in the physical presence of the computer in order to introduce a malicious program. With today's networked computing environments, each computer attached to the Internet is potentially a target for any other computer user on the Internet.

For organizational networks and personal computers, the first layer of security is ensuring that only legitimate users have access to an organization's computing resources. Authentication, the act of entering an approved user name and password, is the first line of defense against unauthorized users. Once a user has successfully authenticated to a network, the network operating system will give the user access to the appropriate printers, files, applications and other resources associated with that particular user account. UNIX, Linux, Novell NetWare and Microsoft Windows Server are the most widely used network operating systems (*PC.Com Encyclopedia,* n.d.). Typical network applications include e-mail, printing and controlled access to storage and applications.

Security software

As a general rule, the more people use a computer, the more problems it will have. Files get corrupted, computers catch viruses or some type of malware and the system takes longer and longer to boot up and load programs. There are three primary ways to limit this wear and tear which it has on your computers:

1. Lock your computers down entirely so that users are only allowed to use the applications on the computer and are not allowed to download or install anything on the computer (user permissions on the computer are set as visitor or guest only).

2. Use software that protects against permanent system reconfiguration by allowing users autonomy to download and install documents and applications on the computer, but upon reboot the computer returns to its original state.

3. Computers are just 'imaged', which involves wiping the entire system clean and installing a fresh copy of the operating system and all applications.

The first method (locking computers down) is controlled through existing network software that provides limited access to users. They are only able to use what is already installed on the computer and they are not allowed to install new software or customize existing applications. While this is a good way to protect the integrity of the computer, it is not very user friendly. For example, some applications work better when customized to the needs of the individual and some applications are configured to save files directly on to the computer. The second way (clean computer on reboot) is an ideal solution allowing users to save their work on the computer and even download applications and small plug-ins on the computer, without giving them the ability to effect permanent changes that may adversely impact other users. This is also an effective solution against software viruses and other malware. The third option (reimaging) pushes a fresh software installation periodically to all computers through the network. This allows users autonomy in using the computers and is a less expensive option than number 2 (which requires individual licences). But reimaging occurs periodically rather than upon every single reboot, so it makes desktops somewhat more vulnerable.

Malware (spyware, viruses, worms, etc.)

Malware, a term for a number of different types of malicious software, can be defined simply as, 'software designed to interfere with a computer's normal functioning' (*Merriam-Webster Online Dictionary*, n.d.(d)). Whereas most software is designed to increase the user's productivity, malware is designed explicitly to perform some type of malicious activity. Malware can be broken into six main categories (May, 2009):

1. *Spyware*: This is some of the newest malware that is particularly dangerous because it is designed to run undetected and report

information about the computer, user activity, user information, etc. back to its creator.

2. *Adware*: This is software that displays pop-up advertisements on the infected computer.

3. *Virus*: This is software that is designed to infect, grow and spread throughout targeted files both on a computer and a network. Viruses are contracted by opening an infected document or executable file, which then infects the compromised computer.

4. *Worms*: Similar to viruses, a worm also replicates itself quickly over a network once it gains access. The difference is that worms are contracted by security holes in your computer's browsers without having to download or open an infected file. In other words, you can get infected by just connecting to the Internet or compromised network.

5. *Trojan*: Named after the infamous Trojan Horse of legend, Trojans hide behind regular software in use and therefore are hard to find. In addition, Trojans are usually designed to inflict damage rather than just annoy.

6. *Cookies*: These are legitimate files used by websites to remember user-IDs and passwords and other previous user behaviour. These can be used to improve the web browsing experience. But some websites place cookies on your computer's browsers designed to seek out information about your user preferences, personal information housed in other cookies, etc.

One of the most frequently asked questions is, 'Are Macs less likely to get a malware?' The simple answer is – yes and no. The answer is yes on two fronts: The Mac operating system is inherently more difficult to attach to than the Microsoft operating system and is also less likely to be targeted than Microsoft systems. However, as Macs have gained market share, there has been an increase in malware designed specifically for them. While Macs are less likely to get viruses, they are certainly not impervious – Apple does recommend that virus protection be used on Macintosh computers.

Hardware and software firewalls

The term 'firewall' comes from a literal brick wall used in apartment complexes to keep a fire from spreading throughout a building. Hardware and software firewalls serve the same function. Hardware firewalls filter all incoming and outgoing traffic in one of three ways (Tyson, 2000):

- packets (each packet of data is compared to the set filters – if approved it is allowed to pass through, if not it is discarded);
- proxy (approved servers outside of the network);
- stateful inspection (analyzes only parts of the data packet and compares it to a database of approved packets).

Where hardware firewalls protect the entire network, software firewalls protect each individual computer. Hardware firewalls can be compromised so it is advisable to also consider having a software firewall. The Microsoft Windows operating system comes with a free software firewall already installed.

Filtering and censorship

One of the best things about the Internet is that it provides free and open access to all kinds of materials and content. Unfortunately, that is also one of the worst things about the Internet. In addition to the global spread of knowledge, the Internet has provided a platform for materials that raise questions of appropriate content, control, filtering and censorship. Internet filters are similar to firewalls in that they block unwanted data from reaching your computer. But in this case they operate by seeking to block content by some combination of domain name, IP address, key word, page content and/or file type (Houghton-Jan, 2010). These Internet filters can be placed on each computer or can oversee the entire network. Internet search engines and websites also can work with countries to block certain content from being accessed by the citizens of that nation. Clearly, there is a fine line between filtering potentially offensive content and outright censorship.

Open access to explicitly violent or pornographic adult content is one of the most controversial issues in libraries. Should children be allowed to freely access any website via library- or other public-supported and government-supported computers? Should adults be allowed to openly view and print this content in a public setting? The Children's Online Privacy Protection Act (COPPA) of 1998 was the initial attempt by the federal government to establish guidelines for how to control access to 'obscene' content to children. COPPA mandated that:

> . . . websites either geared toward children or accepting traffic from children were required to implement privacy and protection policies and which further mandated verifiable consent from parents or guardians before child Internet access was granted. In operation at

the start of 2000, COPPA set out to give parents control of what information was collected online from their children and how that information was to be used. Furthermore, for individuals or businesses operating websites for children thirteen years of age and younger, compliance with COPPA was mandatory. (Federal Trade Commission, n.d.; Ott et al., 2010)

In 2000, Congress passed the Children's Internet Protection Act (CIPA) and superseded COPPA seeking 'to protect children from accessing sexually explicit, harmful or obscene content (Sobel, 2003; Jaegar and Yan, 2009) by requiring schools and public libraries to use Internet filters as a condition upon receiving certain federal funding, such as E-rate' (Ott et al., 2010). This requirement for federal funding led to the widespread use of filtering in public libraries and schools across the nation. By 2005, the Department of Education stated that 100 percent of the nation's public schools were CIPA compliant and by 2008 it was estimated that at least 51 percent of all public libraries were also using Internet filtering in compliance with federal requirements (Jaegar and Yan, 2009).

Outside of the legal and civil liberty issues involved with Internet filtering, the two primary technical issues are overblocking (incorrectly blocking something that has not been identified as objectionable) and underblocking (incorrectly not blocking something identified as objectionable). An examination of overall filtering accuracy studies from 2001 to 2008 shows a cumulative accuracy rate of 75 percent, which means that 25 percent of the time the filters did not function properly (Houghton-Jan, 2010). The ALA has been unequivocal in its stance: '. . . any type of restriction on a person's, including a child's, access to any type of content is unacceptable' (ibid.: 25) and 'the use of filtering software by libraries to block access to constitutionally protected speech violates the Library Bill of Rights' (ALA, 2000).

One of the authors recently testified at a county council meeting on this topic and surmised that while keeping obscene content from his children was of paramount concern, blocking that access was better achieved by parental responsibility and user education rather than by simply installing filters on library computers. After all, his children had multi-faceted access to the Internet through their iPod Touches, iPads, cell phones, school computers, friends' computers, gaming devices, home computers, etc. Spending invaluable resources to filter obscene content, given the county's budget deficits, would in his opinion have much lower priority in comparison to ensuring that the library collections continued to be outstanding, current and of interest to his children.

Internet

Out of the close to two billion worldwide Internet users (Figure 3.17), the continent of Asia is ranked number one in terms of total unique users (825 million), followed by Europe (475 million), North America (266 million), South America/Caribbean (205 million), Africa (111 million), Middle East (63 million) and Australia/Oceania regions (21 million) (Internet World Stats, 2010).

In terms of overall percentage of population using the Internet, however, North America was by far the highest at 77.4 percent followed by Australia (61.3 percent) and Europe (58.4 percent) (Figure 3.18).

In terms of growth since 2000 (Figure 3.19), Africa has shown the most significant growth (2,357 percent), followed by the Middle East (1,825 percent) and Latin America/Caribbean (1,033 percent). North America has shown the smallest growth in the past decade having grown only 146 percent since 2000.

What do the worldwide Internet trends tell us? Seven out of every ten people in North America already use the Internet, whereas six out of ten do in Australia and Europe, and only two out of ten do in Africa and Asia. In terms of absolute numbers, however, four out of every ten of the world's Internet users can be found in Asia. The overall numbers are

Figure 3.17 The world's Internet users

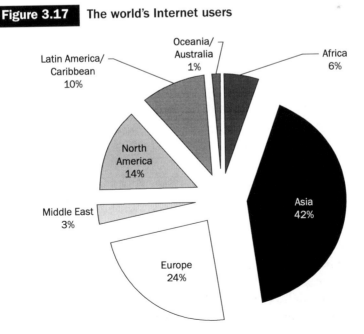

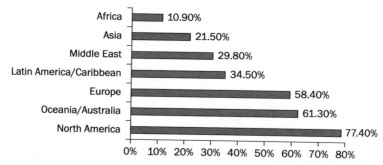

Figure 3.18 Highest Internet market penetration (as a percentage of population)

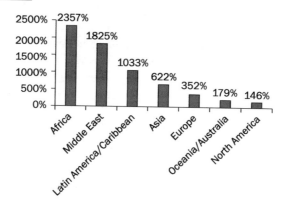

Figure 3.19 Highest growth, 2000–2010

lower in Africa, the Middle East and Latin America, but those regions are seeing an explosion in Internet penetration. Libraries are playing a major role in this expanded access (particularly to underserved populations) and are using this platform to expand their reach to a greater and more diverse population than ever before.

Websites, e-mail and social networking

As of 9 April 2011, the most popular websites on the Internet were Facebook (10.7 percent), Google (7.7 percent), YouTube (3.29 percent), Yahoo! Mail (3.07 percent) and Yahoo (2.4 percent).

As of March 2011, the most popular e-mail programs in the world were Yahoo! Mail (3.07 percent of all web hits), Gmail (1.07 percent), Windows Live Mail (1.00 percent) and AOL mail (0.75 percent). The ability to use e-mail, and train others in its use, has been consistently rated as highly important by library employers. E-mail has become one of the most common ways of communication worldwide.

The top two social networking sites on the web, as of April 2011, account for over 75 percent of all social network site visits. Facebook dominates with a 65 percent market share, with YouTube a distant second at 20 percent. Myspace (1.26 percent), Yahoo! Answers (1.14 percent) and Twitter (1.11 percent) round out the top five most-visited social networking sites (Experian Hitwise, 2011).

Libraries should take note of the popularity of these sites. Because the majority of Internet users can be found on Facebook and YouTube, libraries have an opportunity to use these platforms to reach new users and serve current customers in new ways.

Platform and web browser statistics

In the first quarter of 2011, Windows operating systems accounted for close to 90 percent of all computer platforms worldwide. Macintosh lags far behind but has shown continued growth each year from 4.9 percent in 2008 to 7.97 percent in 2011. Linux is the only other non-Windows operating system to have significant market share at 5.07 percent (*w3schools.com*, 2011) (Figure 3.20).

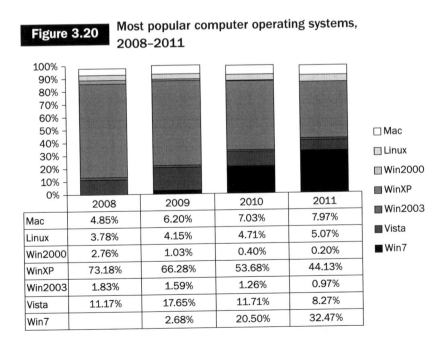

Figure 3.20	Most popular computer operating systems, 2008–2011			
	2008	2009	2010	2011
Mac	4.85%	6.20%	7.03%	7.97%
Linux	3.78%	4.15%	4.71%	5.07%
Win2000	2.76%	1.03%	0.40%	0.20%
WinXP	73.18%	66.28%	53.68%	44.13%
Win2003	1.83%	1.59%	1.26%	0.97%
Vista	11.17%	17.65%	11.71%	8.27%
Win7		2.68%	20.50%	32.47%

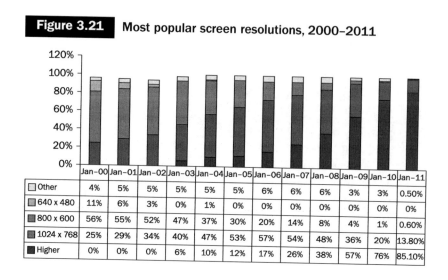

Figure 3.21 Most popular screen resolutions, 2000–2011

	Jan-00	Jan-01	Jan-02	Jan-03	Jan-04	Jan-05	Jan-06	Jan-07	Jan-08	Jan-09	Jan-10	Jan-11
☐ Other	4%	5%	5%	5%	5%	5%	6%	6%	6%	3%	3%	0.50%
▨ 640 x 480	11%	6%	3%	0%	1%	0%	0%	0%	0%	0%	0%	0%
▨ 800 x 600	56%	55%	52%	47%	37%	30%	20%	14%	8%	4%	1%	0.60%
▨ 1024 x 768	25%	29%	34%	40%	47%	53%	57%	54%	48%	36%	20%	13.80%
▨ Higher	0%	0%	0%	6%	10%	12%	17%	26%	38%	57%	76%	85.10%

Screen resolutions (dots per inch) have become increasing smaller as the quality of monitors continues to increase in precision and stability (Figure 3.21). The prevalence of liquid crystal displays or LCD monitors and increasing monitor size has increased the resolution size statically, as LCD monitors are designed for specific screen resolutions (*w3schools.com*, n.d.(a)).

As of March 2011, Firefox is the most popular web browser on the Internet (Figure 3.22). There has been a significant shift in the popularity of web browsers from 2008 to 2011. In 2008, Internet Explorer represented over 50 percent of users but in a three-year span that number has decreased to just over 26 percent. Firefox has surpassed Internet Explorer as the most popular browser but has grown relatively little in popularity overall. Google Chrome has emerged as the third big web browser and will most likely surpass Internet Explorer if the current usage trends continue (*w3schools.com* (n.d.(b))).

Integrated library systems

An integrated library system (ILS) is an enterprise-level software package that manages, integrates and centralizes multiple core library functions and services (Figure 3.23). ILS systems are designed to help libraries with three primary duties: increase operational efficiency, provide access to a library's collection and provide access to external resources

Figure 3.22 Most popular web browsers (2008–2011)

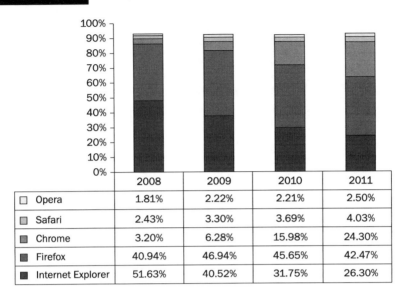

	2008	2009	2010	2011
□ Opera	1.81%	2.22%	2.21%	2.50%
▨ Safari	2.43%	3.30%	3.69%	4.03%
▨ Chrome	3.20%	6.28%	15.98%	24.30%
▨ Firefox	40.94%	46.94%	45.65%	42.47%
■ Internet Explorer	51.63%	40.52%	31.75%	26.30%

Figure 3.23 Integrated library system process

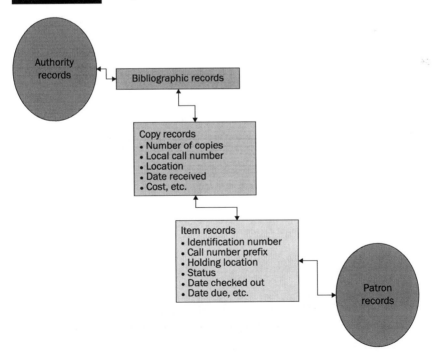

(Kochtanek and Matthews, 2002). ILSs are considered to be the central nervous system of library automation and typically include several discrete but inter-related modules: Acquisitions (for ordering materials); Cataloguing (for generating and managing MARC records); the OPAC (which users utilize to search the catalog); Circulation; and Reserves. The systems are quite complex and bring together a wide variety of records for use in a single transaction. For example, a patron checking out a book might use authority records (the authorized headings that can be used for creating bibliographic records), bibliographic records (i.e. author, series, title, subject headings fields), copy records (one record for each copy of an item in circulation; copy number, location, etc.) and item records (e.g. barcode number, call number, etc.). When a user checks out an item, the ILS links the patron record with the item record, which will keep track of when it is due or past due, the status of the item, etc. (ibid.).

The ILS market still revolves around several large commercial vendors such as SirsiDynix, Ex Libris and Innovative Interfaces, but open source software ILSs such as Koha and Evergreen are starting to gain greater acceptance, particularly among small to mid-size libraries (Breeding, 2011). The focus of the latest generation of ILSs is on cloud computing and on leveraging web layers to manage digital collections from external sources as part of a library's expanded web services.

Databases

A database can be defined as 'a usually large collection of data organized especially for rapid search and retrieval (as by a computer)' (*Merriam-Webster Online Dictionary*, n.d.(e)). ILSs use complex relational databases that store information in tables which allow for cross-referencing with other related tables through common data housed in table rows and columns. A flat database file (as exemplified by a single Excel spreadsheet) lacks the sophistication and power necessary for most ILS functions. Library employers often mention that today's students need to understand database structures – not because they would be expected to create a complex database from scratch, but because an understanding of data structures enhances an employee's ability to work within an ILS to manage content, extract data and run reports.

Here's an example of how a relational database works using J.K. Rowling's first Harry Potter book, *Harry Potter and the Philosopher's Stone*:

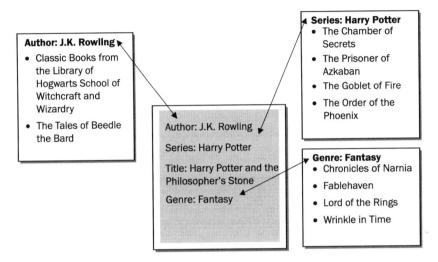

Now the database is able to pull up different records by author, series and genre.

Digitization

The Cornell University Library defines digital imaging as:

> Electronic snapshots taken of a scene or scanned from documents, such as photographs, manuscripts, printed texts and artwork; the digital image is sampled and mapped as a grid of dots or picture elements (pixels). Each pixel is assigned a tonal value (black, white, shades of gray or color), which is represented in binary code (zeros and ones). The binary digits ('bits') for each pixel are stored in a sequence by a computer and often reduced to a mathematical representation (compressed). The bits are then interpreted and read by the computer to produce an analog version for display or printing. (Jones, 2001)

Digitization, at its most basic definition, is the act of taking a physical item and making it computer-readable (Schlumpf, 2007). According to the Institute of Library and Museum Services (IMLS, 2006: 1):

> The use of technology and particularly digital technology has affected nearly every aspect of library and museum services, from the automation of internal cataloguing and management systems to the digitization of physical collections, and from the acquisition of

new 'borndigital' works of art and library publications to the use of technology to present collections and engage audiences.

The IMLS report found that public libraries' nationwide digitization priorities were focused on the digitization of historical records and archives (50.5 percent), photographs (31.7 percent) and newspapers (28.8 percent) and that their primary challenges focused on funding and resources to complete their planned digitization priorities. For academic libraries, their priorities focused on digitization of historical documents/ archives (38.7 percent), course material (33.9 percent) and photographs (24.2 percent). As with public libraries, challenges for academic libraries include lack of staff and time and other competing higher priority projects.

Most libraries view digitization as an area of librarianship poised for explosive growth. Digitization of unique library collections will increase and require a larger share of resources as digital projects make hidden and underused special collections available to researchers worldwide. As Clifford Lynch (Coalition for Networked Information) has said, 'special collections are a nexus where technology and content are meeting to advance scholarship in extraordinary new ways' (ACRL Research Planning and Review Committee, 2010: 288).

Software profiles of our case studies

The software and databases are where the libraries significantly differ, which is to be expected based on their differing user bases. While the computing software is similar (Windows, Microsoft Office, security software), the academic library has more specialized productivity and Web 2.0 software and access to a far greater number of databases. The public library focuses more on professional development, specialty areas of interest (e.g. antiques and ancestry) and youth services. The school library is focused more on media services and production and online learning within the context of instructional technology.

At each type of library, users utilize technology to meet their information needs. They will generally use whatever technology the library makes available, which to some extent means that the technology drives the usage. But all libraries would like their equipment to reflect their service community's information technology needs. This presents us with a classic 'which comes first, the chicken or the egg?' scenario. We know that ensuring a robust, well maintained technology infrastructure is essential, but it can be difficult to ascertain which particular elements are in most need of attention.

The organization's strategic plan (along with current usage patterns of users) will help guide decisions around why and how technology can help meet the needs of users. Let us go back to our example goal from Chapter 2, 'Goal 1: A vibrant, user-centered collection'. How can technology help with meeting this essential organizational goal? Both the words 'vibrant' and 'user-centered' can be supported by technology as they denote opportunities for expanded information access. So how does a library know if its collection is considered 'vibrant' by its users? One way is to provide multiple ways for users to access and experience its collection. Some public libraries create virtual libraries in virtual worlds so users can experience collections in three-dimensional virtual spaces; another possibility would be leveraging social networking so users could discuss controversial, popular, or just relevant aspects of its collection. Technology could also assist in making the collection more 'user-centered' through its ILS, online surveys, polling, blogs and being offered in different formats such as through e-books and in different formats such as audio, movie, etc.

The good news is that most of this technology is available for free or at little cost. The planning and resource allocation in terms of staff time and resources, however, are not. The key point to note, however, is that technology provides many ways for an organization to achieve its stated goals, many of which are cost effective. How do you know what you most need and whether or not it is working?

The next step, once you have identified your priority goals, is to identify and customize access to your collection based on the users that the organization is trying to serve. College students differ from the faculty that teach them, public library users come from all different racial, ethnic, socio-economic and generational backgrounds, and school libraries deal with a wide range of subjects, disciplines and users from a wide range of ages.

Are the primary users the organization seeks to serve predominately from a specific demographic? If so, then it is a relatively easy task to customize interfaces and user to meet the needs of a specific target audience. For example, a product or online service directed at a public library's youth services department would likely have simplified terminology, more color and larger buttons.

If, as is more likely, a library is seeking to serve a diverse audience, then two approaches are possible. A library may allow its users to self-select their group. For example, a school district website could allow students to select either 'elementary', 'middle school', or 'high school' and then deliver age-appropriate interfaces and resources. A more sophisticated approach requires individual logins in order to provide customized delivery. For example, as a student logs in to a university's online learning system, a library web service could consult online student records and identify her major/minor status and currently enrolled classes and then deliver resources that are most appropriate to her individual needs.

Individualized approaches to information delivery are somewhat analogous to tailor-made suits – they certainly fit better than 'one size fits all' clothing, but are also much more expensive. In many libraries the balance between customized and standardized approaches will largely be determined by budgetary realities.

Software support FAQs

1. What is the best way to protect our computers from malware?

The first of two best ways is to use software like DeepFreeze, which freezes the hard drive so that any changes that occur on the computer will not be saved and will be wiped out upon rebooting the computer. In this way, users have maximum autonomy to download, install and create documents on the computer and even intentionally try and harm the computer, but none of the changes will be kept.

The second option, which is what the majority of people do outside of a general computer lab environment, is to ensure that you have a suite of software (free to personal users) protecting your computer from malware – software firewall (comes with Windows), virus protection and spyware/ad aware protection (some software covers all three and some focuses on only one).

2. Our computers are running slowly, what should we do?

When a computer is running slowly it usually means that its available resources are being maximized, which causes it to process new requests slowly because it is already processing other information. There are several potential causes of this: not enough RAM available to handle the software you are running (that is the standard software you are running requires more RAM to run simultaneously with other software programs); malware activity where processes not authorized by you are taking place in the background (check the activity of your computer by pressing ctrl + alt + delete on a Windows machine); or you may simply have too many software applications running at the same time.

3. *As an MLIS student, what software should I be expected to be familiar with when I enter the field?*

Of course, this is a moving target. An IMLS study in 2006 showed that, both for public and academic libraries, staff just need to be familiar with the technologies being provided to and used by users. These include desktop, laptop and tablet computers; wireless connectivity; software running the computers and printers; network connectivity; e-mail; databases, especially the ILS being used; office productivity software; web browsers; RFID technology; and other multi-media hardware and software being loaned out to users.

The bottom line is: you have to become familiar with the technology the library is using to serve users and the technology users are bringing into the library. Learn by using the technology itself.

4

Technology and budgeting

Abstract: Technology is expensive. How often should technology be replaced? This chapter discusses the basic budgeting process, the core concepts behind them such as 'prevention vs. reaction', 'quality vs. quantity', and 'replacement vs. repair'. How to prioritize and the current budgeting trends for libraries are also discussed.

Key words: budgeting, technology, zero-sum, line-item, prevention, prioritizing, trends, quality, quantity, replacement.

There are many different approaches to information technology budgeting: prevention vs. reaction, quality vs. quantity, replacement vs. repair and zero-sum vs. line item budgeting. All technologies should be considered consumables that will require consistent maintenance and repair and eventual replacement. Although the cost of any given item (e.g. a laptop) has declined from year to year, library IT budgets have grown significantly because libraries are buying and supporting an ever-increasing range and number of technologies. There are three ways to look at information technology and budgeting within an organization (Dougherty, 2009):

- *as a driver and necessity* (so funds are given a priority and cut less than other departments);

- *as a cost center* (so funds are cut more than other departments because its budget is so much larger);

- *as an equal to other departments* (funds are treated equally to other departments).

Our view is that technology certainly should be viewed as *a driver and necessity* as it represents the core foundation of an organization's infrastructure.

Prevention vs. reaction

Library technology decision-making should be considered an exercise in risk management. Risk cannot be eliminated (there will always be failures and unexpected system 'down time'), but we can use preventative techniques to limit our risks. The two most common approaches to risk mitigation are replacing technology on a frequent basis so that it does not get too old or worn down and/or having a robust warranty and repair plan so that when there is a technology failure it is addressed immediately. The difficulty with applying a prevention strategy is that it costs a considerable amount upfront and means replacing technology that is in reasonable working condition based on an arbitrary schedule rather than whether it actually needs to be replaced at any given time. With today's tight budgets, it can be hard to justify discarding a machine that still seems to be performing acceptably. The return on investment (ROI), however, for adopting a scheduled replacement strategy is very high in terms of money, time, stress and overall satisfaction of users and employees.

Computers typically are on a three-year replacement cycle; that is, a computer should be replaced after its third year, sometime early during its fourth year of use. Why? Some suggest that computer manufacturers purposefully engineer computer parts to last only three years. Conspiracy theories aside, however, a functioning computer utilizes a large number of physical components that all must work well together in order for it to be functional – power supply that is plugged into the wall for electricity, mother board that connects all other electronic parts together, processing chip, hard drive, video/graphic/sound cards, CD drive, keyboard, mouse, monitor, etc. As with anything else, if they are used frequently and often then something will invariably stop working. When a computer is replaced, typically this means everything with it including monitor, mouse and keyboard.

Another primary rationale is that technology ages quickly in terms of performance and capacity to run software designed for more robust machines. For example, when considering the Windows operating system alone, each newer version of the operating system has required more RAM (called the memory footprint) to operate the computer, although

Windows 2007 has slightly bucked this trend in comparison to Windows Vista. The same is true with other productivity software. For example, Microsoft Office requirements doubled in both RAM and processing speed from Office 2003 to Office 2007 (Microsoft, 2010). With these two software applications alone, the need for more processing speed and RAM has substantially increased. Add in an e-mail client, trying to download and upload files and other changing software requirements such as video and graphic rendering, and clearly trying to run newer software on older hardware becomes painfully slow or not possible at all. If you were designing software would you design it for the specifications of newer or older potentially outdated hardware?

The alternative to the proactive replacement strategy is waiting and reacting after the point of failure. It is tempting to save money on replacement costs by waiting until systems break down, but this approach entails three significant hidden costs. First, waiting until something breaks means that the library has, and becomes associated with, broken information technology equipment or services (perhaps several at any given time!). The impact on the user is immediate and negative. He or she is unable to use the library catalog, search a database, or meet some other important need. The user becomes frustrated and their impression of the library suffers. Unfortunately, these failures often cause 'ripple effects' that spread far beyond a single user. In a library setting, many failures may go unreported, which means the problem remains unresolved until after it has affected multiple users. And, even after being reported, problems may take some time to resolve, rendering important library services and equipment 'out of order' for lengthy periods.

Second, while it may seem fiscally prudent to squeeze as much use as possible out of library technology (i.e. keep machines in service until they fail), this approach leads to budgetary uncertainties that can far outweigh any cost savings. Libraries that have a standard replacement schedule know exactly what their costs will be over time. But waiting for failures could mean significant costs at unpredictable times and can lead to situations in which a core service fails at a time when no money is available for replacement.

Third, cyclical ordering of equipment is much more efficient than ordering hardware one at a time as things break. Libraries can often get discounts on bulk orders. In addition, ordering lots of equipment at once means that the library can procure identical pieces of equipment, which will save significant IT staff time in terms of equipment maintenance. The more hardware profiles a library has at any given time, the higher the support costs.

In a worst-case scenario, a reactive approach to technology planning snowballs into a situation where the organization spends most of its time and energy reacting and 'putting out fires' as opposed to planning and preventing; like a large ripple on a pond, reacting to technology failure reverberates throughout the organization leaving uncertainty and dissonance in its wake.

Quality vs. quantity

Choosing quality over quantity means purchasing technology not because it is at the lowest price but because it represents quality, not from a strictly name brand perspective, but it terms of performance, customer support and maintenance agreements. This concept goes hand-in-hand with the tenet of prevention vs. reaction.

Quality costs money, however, and not only will the unit costs be more expensive but adding in the maintenance plans will add even more to the total cost of each technology device. This limits the total number of units an organization can purchase. The valued added, however, is significant. The organization that purchases 'quality' technology will have equipment that should have higher performance, fewer failures and less down-time. The proverbial ripple effect is small, leaving a relatively calm, placid technology infrastructure; it is often said that the best technology infrastructure is the one that remains completely invisible and seamless. Users do what they need to do and then move on without consciously thinking about the technology they are using.

Replacement vs. repair

The Florida Governor's IT director had a 25 percent replacement cycle every year. In this fashion, every employee received a new computer during the fourth year of use, the overall cost was managed and the line item of the budget ensured that the resources were always available. Other organizations simply track the purchase date of computers and replace them after three years have expired. Maintenance warranties, not coincidentally, typically last only three years, with the understanding that the likelihood of computer parts failing after three years is much higher and much costlier to the computer manufacturers. These organizations practice the strategy of replacement over repair where computers rarely fail, which provides a stable technology foundation and removes the likelihood of older hardware and new software requirement incompatibility problems.

Organizations that still live by the 'if it isn't broken, then don't fix it' mindset will find that a computer will always break at the most inopportune times and usually while someone is operating it. This presents the worst-case scenario for users, maximizing their frustration and magnifying the effect of the failure. Doing diagnostics on a failed machine will take time and resources and, even if it can be repaired, will require expedited ordering and then more maintenance time once the part arrives. Again, the footprint of such events is large and deep. While the overall cost of one instance is not great, the impact it has in terms of morale, time and resource allocation is major. Each additional failure increases this magnitude of impact.

Zero-sum vs. line-item budgeting

Budgeting for technology is not much different to budgeting for other organizational resources. The two primary types of budgets are *zero-sum* and *line-item* budgeting. *Zero-sum* budgeting emphasizes priorities and needs and is developed around what is projected rather than what has been funded in the past. *Line-item* budgeting shows the cost of all resources but is organized based on type of resource rather than priority. From a budgeting standpoint, especially when budget cuts are a possibility or there is a need for justification, zero-sum budgets are more helpful. Let us take a look at a hypothetical zero-sum budget from a technology budgeting standpoint.

Zero-sum budgeting

This type of budgeting has requested resources organized by recurring and then priority order. Priority one are the 'must-haves' and are the highest priority, priority two are the 'would like to haves' and are medium priorities, and priority three are the 'would be nice to haves' and are the lowest priorities. To start building your zero-sum technology budget, start with the recurring costs first. In Table 4.1, our public library example, computers were leased, so let us use them as our example:

Table 4.1   Recurring costs

A public library example budget			
Recurring annual costs 2011–2012			
Item	Cost ($)	Units/Month	Total ($)
Networking services*	2,000.00	12	24,000.00
Computers*	300.00	130	39,000.00
Printing services*	200.00	12	2,400.00
Database 1	10.00	12	120.00
Database 2	20.00	12	240.00
Database 3	15.00	12	180.00
Database 4	40.00	12	480.00
Database 5	10.00	12	120.00
Database 6	3.00	12	36.00
Database 7	4.00	12	48.00
Database 8	9.00	12	108.00
Database 9	7.00	12	84.00
Database 10	2.00	12	24.00
		Recurring TOTAL	66,840.00

* Annual Lease

The library's annual recurring operating technology budget is $66,840.00 and includes networking services, leased computers, printing services and database subscriptions (if annual lease, divide by 12 to get monthly cost).

In Table 4.2, we take a look at a prioritized list of other technology needs.

The total requested budget for the next fiscal year is $84,050.00 and, after adding $66,840.00 for recurring costs, the total requested technology budget is $150,890.00 for 2011–2012. Notice that the requested budget is organized by priority, with the top priority items occurring first and the lowest priority items listed last.

Using Excel for budgeting

Microsoft Excel is an excellent software application to use for budgeting purposes because it is extremely easy and usually available and readable

Table 4.2 Requested budget

Requested 2011–2012 technology budget				
Item	Cost ($)	Units/Month	Total ($)	Priority	Comments
Self-checkout stations	16,000.00	3	48,000.00	1	Research shows a cost savings of up to 30%.
RFID system	3,000.00	1	3,000.00	1	Computer that reads and processes RFID tags.
RFID tags	0.07	50000	3,500.00	1	Individual RFID tags to attach to library resources.
Microsoft 2010 software	100.00	120	12,000.00	1	Current machines have 2003 and integration issues have become a frequent complaint.
54' LCD screens	2,000.00	2	4,000.00	2	Display boards to mount at entrances of floors two and three.
e-Book database	100.00	12	1,200.00	2	Request to expand e-book holdings increased by 50% over the past year.
Laptops	1,500.00	5	7,500.00	2	Replacements for five laptops for checkout are no longer functional and out of warranty.
54' LCD screens	2,000.00	2	4,000.00	3	Display boards to mount at entrances of floors two and three.
Webcams	30.00	15	450.00	3	Staff has reported a desire for video conferencing capability.
Flash drives	20.00	20	400.00	3	Portable and inexpensive way to store and manage data.
Requested Priority 1			66,500.00		
Requested Priority 2			2,700.00		
Requested Priority 3			4,850.00		
Total Requested			**84,050.00**		

by most people and computers. Here is a quick primer on how to use Excel to create this exemplar budget quickly and easily. Feel free to recreate this and follow along using Excel for some hands-on practice. Let us start with explaining the basic layout of Excel and how to create some basic formulas for addition and multiplication.

Excel is a spreadsheet program that is divided by columns (letters) and rows (numbers). While all of the menu items can be disorienting, the majority are not needed to create a basic budget. Figure 4.1 illustrates some of its basic functions within the context of the example budget.

Figure 4.2 shows how you can create headings for your table: Item, Cost, Units/Month and Total. Notice they are centered both horizontally and vertically.

The two primary formulas to be used are 'add' and 'multiply', and the key is to let Excel know which cells to work with. Create an equation either in the function area or by selecting the 'sum all' Greek symbol 'Σ', which is located to the top right corner of the Home menu. Figure 4.3 shows how the cost for networking services over a 12-month period can be calculated quickly. In addition, once the equation is set, Excel will automatically repeat that equation for the next one if copied.

Figure 4.1 Creating a budget in Excel

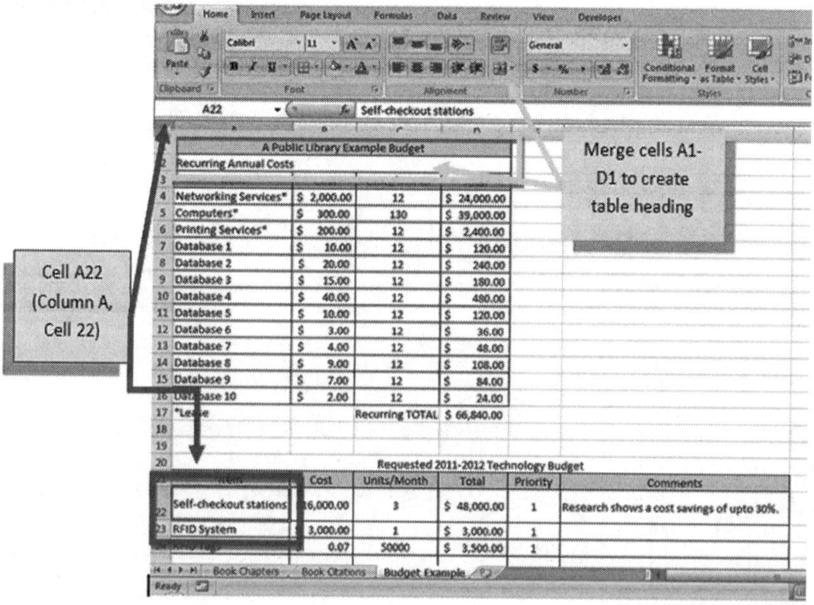

Figure 4.2 Centering text in Excel

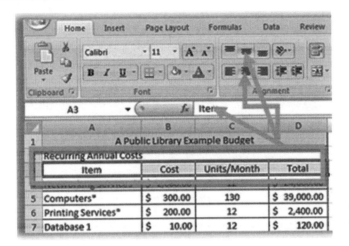

Figure 4.3 Excel multiplication formula

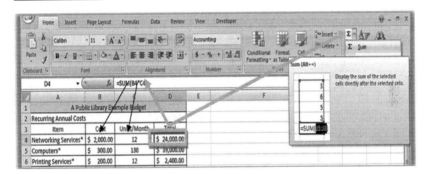

By copying the equation just created and pasting it, Excel will recreate the formula for a new row. In the example in Figure 4.4, the column 'Computers' is automatically calculated when the formula for networking services is pasted. Note the cell numbers multiplied automatically increase by one from B4 to B5. This can be repeated for all additional budget categories.

The formula for 'adding' cells is even easier. Consecutive cells can be added by selecting the cells and separating them with a colon as shown in Figure 4.5. In this case it is D4:D16 to total the recurring costs.

To add different cells, for example subtotals from recurring and requested, separate the cells using a comma as in Figure 4.6.

Figure 4.4 Excel repeats pasted formulas

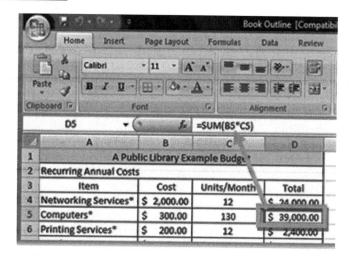

Figure 4.5 Adding numbers in Excel

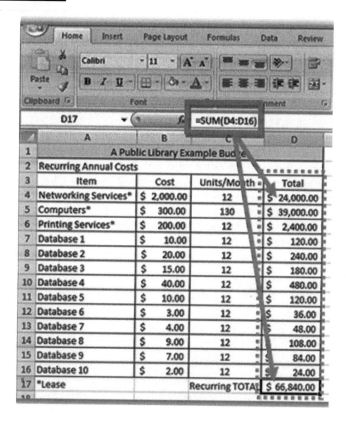

Figure 4.6   Adding subtotals in Excel

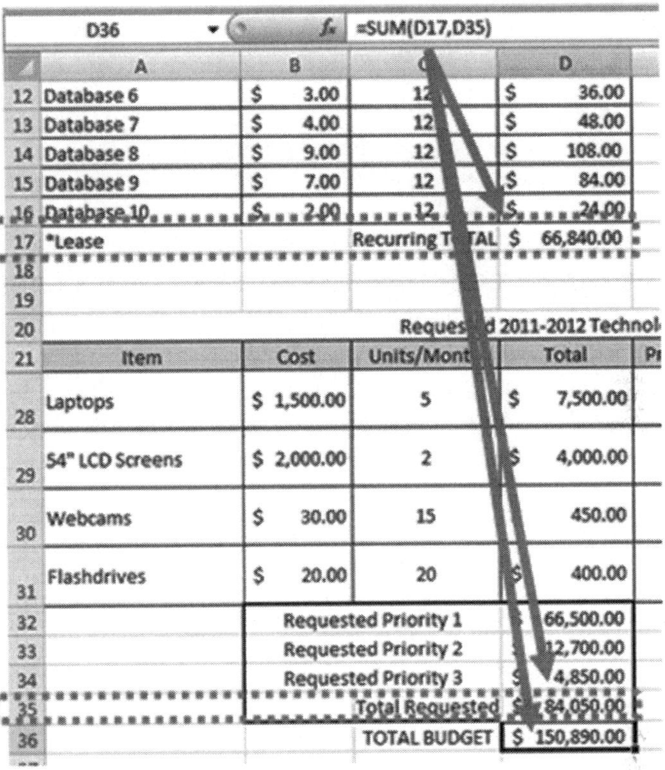

	D36		f_x	=SUM(D17,D35)	
	A	**B**	**C**	**D**	
12	Database 6	$ 3.00	12	$ 36.00	
13	Database 7	$ 4.00	12	$ 48.00	
14	Database 8	$ 9.00	12	$ 108.00	
15	Database 9	$ 7.00	12	$ 84.00	
16	Database 10	$ 2.00	12	$ 24.00	
17	*Lease		Recurring TOTAL	$ 66,840.00	
18					
19					
20			Request d 2011-2012 Technol		
21	**Item**	**Cost**	**Units/Mont**	**Total**	**Pr**
28	Laptops	$ 1,500.00	5	$ 7,500.00	
29	54" LCD Screens	$ 2,000.00	2	$ 4,000.00	
30	Webcams	$ 30.00	15	450.00	
31	Flashdrives	$ 20.00	20	400.00	
32			Requested Priority 1	66,500.00	
33			Requested Priority 2	12,700.00	
34			Requested Priority 3	4,850.00	
35			Total Requested	84,050.00	
36			TOTAL BUDGET	$ 150,890.00	

The inherent values of keeping an electronic budget in a spreadsheet are:

- Calculations are automatic, thereby increasing accuracy.
- Saving and sharing with others is quick and easy.
- Numbers and totals can be edited and changed quickly and accurately.
- Tables can be charted, graphed and placed in reports easily.
- Multiple budgets can be linked and followed simultaneously.

Prioritizing technology

How to prioritize what technology should be funded first? A good analogy would be a car. What are the most critical major components? The engine, of course – without this the car will be unable to move – and how powerful the engine is will largely determine how fast you can go. Another central component would the car's tyres. If one is flat, regardless of how powerful the engine, the car cannot move. Another major component is the gas – without fuel to consume, the engine cannot operate and the car will remain idle.

The routers (connect organization to ISP Internet connection), switches (connection points to organization's computers), servers (maintains the website and other software applications) and wireless access points (assuming a wireless environment) are the components that comprise the engine. Computers are the tyres, and network bandwidth (how much of it is being licensed from the ISP) is the gas. Collectively, how functional and powerful the organization's routers, switches, servers and wireless connectivity are will determine how powerfully its engine or capacity for networked services can perform. Regardless of the engine's capacity, if the tyres are flat or non-functional or, in other words, the organization's computers are non-functional or cannot handle the network capacity, then users will be unable to perform their desired tasks at a high level on a consistent basis. And, regardless of how powerful the car's engine and how well maintained its tyres are, without gas or network connectivity (enough bandwidth to handle the volume of network traffic throughout the organization) all network activity (running software applications like Microsoft Office, connecting to the Internet, printing, opening e-mail) will move slowly or not work at all.

The other tenet to remember is prevention over reaction, which means frequent checkups for the car to make sure all of its working parts are in order. In terms of budgeting for technology, this means making sure that the network components, computers and network bandwidth are well taken care of and well funded *before* problems occur. This means paying for enough bandwidth before slowdowns occur for employees and users, which means ensuring network components (which often have a longer life span than traditional computers) and desk top computers are under warranty, well maintained and replaced on a regular basis, which in turn means fixing what is not broken rather than waiting for them to fail before doing something. This means that in an annual budget spread across three years, funding for replacements to End of Service (EOS) technology should be considered and planned for.

Dugan (2002) proposes an eight-point information technologies cost model to keep in mind:

1. *Investigation:* Initial research that will need to be conducted (staff time).

2. *Negotiation:* Measured in terms of potential savings such as through a consortium or long-term contract.

3. *Acquisition:* Moving forward with either the purchase or the lease.

4. *Installation:* Integrating the technology into your organization.

5. *Training:* Orienting staff and patrons (if applicable) to the new technology.

6. *Maintenance:* Ensuring technology remains functional and usable.

7. *Evaluation:* Identifying and collecting appropriate metrics to determine impact and outcomes of technology.

8. *Upgrades or replacement:* When, and should the technology be upgraded or replaced?

Budgeting trends

> More libraries saw budget decreases in 2010 than budget increases, but budgets are expected to level out in 2011. Despite news reports of budget-strapped local municipalities cutting services to the bone, the survey found that community public libraries outpaced academic and other libraries in spending increases. (McKendrick, 2011)

In 2010, in direct response to the global economic downturn, library budgets across the country were for the most part reduced. This has created a 'perfect storm' where 'while library use soared, a majority of states reported cuts in state funding to public libraries and to the state library agencies that support libraries and statewide library programs' (ALA, 2010: i). Despite the onset of this perfect storm, a recent survey of 1,201 of the nation's library directors suggests they are finding creative ways not only of weathering the storm but even of providing new programming through alternative funding sources (McKendrick, 2011).

The average library budget ranges from $800,000 to $3 million and the nationwide survey found that 'community public libraries actually outpaced academic and other libraries in spending increases' (ibid.: 3) and that the budget cuts, instead of cutting services, have led to a shift in short-term funding priorities where material and staff travel budgets have been cut while salaries are frozen and the move to digitizing collections and online database subscriptions have increased. Funding and technology are the two top concerns for surveyed managers over the next five years and 'respondents were also keenly aware of the need to not only keep pace with technology and operate like a business, but also clearly communicate the value of libraries to their constituents; community support and involvement is a bedrock practice that is vital as libraries enter the digital age' (ibid.: 4).

The positive news, however, is that the majority of library directors feel that the worst of the economic downturn has been weathered and also the fact that many of the library users tend to be 5–10 years behind the technology curve, and therefore there is time to ensure that the technology being provided is meeting their needs appropriately. As one survey respondent puts it, 'the fact is that a large majority of the population still remains 5–10 years or more behind the technology in regard to training and being able to comfortably utilize the range of technology available. The need for digital transliteracy is becoming more apparent with the high unemployment and upcoming career opportunities. Libraries are [in a] position to meet that need and others' (ibid.: 4).

5

Evaluation: is technology meeting the needs of the organization's users?

Abstract: How do you know whether your technology infrastructure is meeting the needs of your users? This chapter goes in-depth on how to evaluate your organization's performance through a variety of methods and identifying and collecting relevant data and information necessary to make informed, strategic choices. Concepts such as informatics and building a logic model for new programming are discussed with hands-on examples provided.

Key words: evaluation, formative, summative, informatics, evaluation method, logic model, outcomes-based evaluation.

There are multiple ways to explore whether an organization's technology is meeting the needs of its users: usage statistics, user complaints, technology performance data, user surveys, focus groups, interviews, etc. The key is to have a system in place for evaluating the overall efficacy of the organization's technology infrastructure with an emphasis on prevention and continuous improvement. From a systems standpoint, evaluation is a continuous process and represents the final stage in the ADDIE process. Evaluation starts with the desired ends (are they clearly defined and measured?) and then works backwards to determine whether the necessary means (are they clearly defined and measured?) are being allocated in an efficient and effective fashion.

Formative and summative evaluation

Formative evaluation is designed to measure the impact of something while it is taking place and allows for incremental improvements to occur in a 'just in time' fashion. From an input/output standpoint this means measuring the quality of the inputs (components and the whole system) before measuring the outputs (the impact of the whole system) with the logic being that quality 'inputs' will lead to quality 'outputs'. Formative evaluation in terms of technology could be customer satisfaction surveys of both employees and users in terms of computing services; an analysis of whether all computers are under warranty or which ones need to replaced; and interviews with management, employees and technology support staff about the efficacy of the technology system in general.

Summative evaluation focuses on the outputs and short-term and long-term impact or outcomes. The focus is on the ends themselves – have they been attained? Are they even being measured? If the ends have not been attained, what are the reasons? The longer-term impact or outcomes focuses on the meaning of the technology for users and employees – are they being more productive? Are the career databases being utilized more and are users finding jobs? Are the youth computers being used more and, if so, for what and how are they being used? From a funding standpoint, in particular, summative evaluation helps pinpoint the 'value-added' of the organization's technology infrastructure.

Bertot suggests a 'service quality and outcomes assessment' paradigm where:

> Libraries need to know what investments (inputs) produce what services (outputs) in order to determine the perceived quality (quality assessment) and impacts (outcomes) of those services/resources. Depending on the assessed outcome and quality, library managers will want to modify their resource investment to attempt to achieve, or sustain, the desired service outcome(s). (Bertot, 2003: 214)

From a resource allocation standpoint, the ability to determine which resources are most used, asked for and assist with the greatest efficiency and effectiveness towards attainment of the library's long-term outcomes (goals) will allow decisions using limited funds to be as precise and accurate as possible. The use of informatics, discussed below, is especially helpful here.

Hiller and Self (2004: 132) suggest considering evaluations at both the macro and micro levels. Macroevaluation

> measures how well a system operates and the results usually can be expressed in quantitative terms (e.g., percentage of success in satisfying requests for interlibrary loans).

Microevaluation

> investigates how a system operates and why it operates at a particular level. Because it deals with factors affecting the performance of the system, microevaluation is necessary if the results of the investigation will, in some way, be used to improve performance.

Informatics

The concept of informatics involves collecting the data needed to make informed decisions about a system or service. Several fundamental tenets must be in play for informatics to be collected and used in a meaningful way – data collection must be automated, just-in-time, relevant and digestible by management so it can make informed, strategic decisions about its performance. From a technology standpoint, this means its informatics involve such data as bandwidth usage, database usage, website and page hit counts, computer and other technology usage, user access (through logins), number of complaints and replacement cycles.

Collecting such data in an automated, real-time fashion takes a lot of planning but allows an organization to make quick, strategically-effective decisions about how best to use an always-limited budget towards maintaining a strong technology infrastructure. What databases are being used and which are not? Which computers are being used more in which part of the library, and for what purpose (determines what software to potentially upgrade)? Where are the user complaints coming from and how can these gaps be closed?

Policies, guidelines and management software help ensure the necessary data is being collected at all times. Software for routers can be purchased that 'manages' them so that overall bandwidth to various parts of the organization is always monitored and can be directed accordingly. Purchase and replacement dates represent a manual process of data entry at the time of sale into a database or spreadsheet. User complaints can either be tracked automatically using ticket tracking software or again manually by employees. Website hit counts can be monitored using various web tracking software (e.g. Google Analytics) and database hits are usually tracked by the vendors themselves and are readily shared with the organization.

Evaluation method

There are two, overarching types of evaluation method: qualitative and quantitative. Qualitative methods involve interviews, observations, focus groups, collecting documentation about the organization and surveys focused on understanding the context of an organization through descriptive text and nominal data or data that can be arranged into categories that are arbitrary in nature. For example, after a series of interviews, the qualitative data suggests that the employees are satisfied with their technology because three of the four interviews used words such as 'very satisfied', 'no complaints', and 'excellence'. Observations of employees and users were also favorable as both groups engaged with the technology and performed their tasks seamlessly without interruption. The technology seemed well maintained. Focus groups with both users and employees suggest that, in general, they are very satisfied with the organization's technology and are consistently able to perform their tasks at a high level and without interruption. Documentation shows all computers are under warranty and have three-year replacement cycles. The wireless access points are using the most current wireless connectivity standard. Annual survey data also support the overall perception that users and employees are extremely satisfied with the organization's technology infrastructure.

Quantitative methods focus on collecting data dealing with numbers that are ordinal (rankings) and interval data (ratings and frequency counts). Typical quantitative methods are pretty much the same but data is collected into numerical data-structured interviews, survey ratings and rankings. Typical quantitative data include usage statistics, survey ratings (e.g. why do you use the library?) and satisfaction ratings (e.g. 75 percent of users surveyed were satisfied).

Which is the best way to go? While there has been an historical argument over which is a better way to understand reality, contemporary thinking largely suggests that both qualitative (why) and quantitative data (what and how much) should be collected. For example, on a survey, if 75 percent of respondents are 'unsatisfied' you want to know why they are not satisfied. If access to a database has gone up by 50 percent over a year's time, you want to talk to users about why this is the case. Although input measures have been collected in libraries since the early 1900s, only in the 1990s have output measures been collected and not in a systematic fashion centered around users (Kyrillidou, 2002) and their needs, perspectives and satisfaction levels. While Kyrillidou suggests multiple measurement models such as the Linear model (input–output–quality–outcome), the Cyclic model (same variables but instead of being linear, that is step-by-step in a sequence, they are interrelated), or the Spiral Swirl model (users and library interactions with each other create a 'motion' that must be measured within the context of the same variables), the bottom line is that evaluation must be consistent and performed frequently on the entire system at both macro and micro levels. Both formative and summative data will provide the organization with the data necessary to make informed decisions about its future by ensuring clear and tight alignment between organizational ends (outputs and outcomes) and means (inputs necessary to attain the ends). While it is tempting to try and measure everything, which often leads to being overwhelmed and to general inertia, the key to quality organizational evaluation is that it is consistent, longitudinal, focused on both inputs and outputs and reported in such a fashion that management can make real-time decisions about the future.

Building a logic model for outcomes-based evaluation

> The logic modelling process makes explicit what is often implicit. Also, if done carefully, the process lays out a 'theory of change', highlighting the plausible pathways through which resources translate into outcomes and identifying mediating factors that can help or hinder success at key points. (Jordan, 2010: 264)

A logic model can be defined as '. . . a picture of how your organization does its work – the theory and assumptions underlying the program. A program logic model links outcomes (both short-term and long-term) with program activities/processes and the theoretical assumptions/principles of the program' (W. K. Kellogg Foundation, 2004: III). Logic models help to maintain focus on the most important goals of programs and services: impact and outcomes on users both in the short term and long term. In essence, it is seeking the rationale for the 'what', 'whom' and 'how' of service delivery. What's the point? On whom will it impact and in what ways? How will it be implemented?

The Institute of Museum and Library Services (IMLS, n.d.) defines a logic model as the overall evaluation plan for outcome-based evaluation (OBE) designed to in a systemic way:

> . . . determine if a program has achieved its goals. The organized process of developing an outcome-based program and a logic model (an evaluation plan) helps institutions articulate and establish clear program benefits (outcomes), identify ways to measure those program benefits (indicators), clarify the specific individuals or groups for which the program's benefits are intended (target audience) and design program services to reach that audience and achieve the desired results.

One of the most important results of developing a logic model is that it 'builds shared understanding of performance expectations' (Jordan, G. B., 2010: 271) within the organization. The rationale for using such a systemic approach is that:

> Current policy and program rationale, objectives and evaluation use a fragmented picture of the innovation process. The analogy was used at one meeting of evaluators on the subject of people who are blindfolded describing an elephant differently depending on what part of the elephant they are touching. Legs may seem like tree trunks and ears like large fans. Without looking at a complete picture of the elephant, it isn't possible to appropriately evaluate how the elephant functions or how various parts contribute to that functioning. Looking at only part of the elephant gives incomplete or incorrect answers. (ibid.: 263)

Using a logic model is especially important when dealing with the diffusion of technology because both the context in which it is implemented and the interaction effect between technology and the users it serves are complex and rapidly changing (Tassey, 2007 as cited in Jordan, 2010).

Developing a logic model starts with the end and works backward to the very beginning. This process is illustrated in Figure 5.1 from right to left.

The 'ends' an organization seeks to attain are identified as *short-term* (less than 3 years) and *long-term* (3 years or more) outcomes, or the

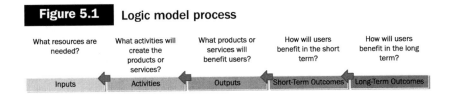

Figure 5.1 Logic model process

Inputs	Activities	Outputs	Short-Term Outcomes	Long-Term Outcomes
What resources are needed?	What activities will create the products or services?	What products or services will benefit users?	How will users benefit in the short term?	How will users benefit in the long term?

'specific changes in program participants' behavior, knowledge, skills, status and level of functioning' (W.K. Kellogg Foundation, 2004: 2) the new product or service intends to achieve. Notice that these outcomes are not articulated in terms of merely providing services for users but rather they are focused on one level above the service level – on how specifically users receiving services will benefit from their use. This is a critical factor that cannot be over-emphasized. *Outputs* are the specific products or services that users receive that are intended to create the value-added short- and long-term outcomes. *Activities* are the tasks that must be done to generate the services and products, and the *Inputs* are the actual resources that are required to begin this entire chain reaction (Figure 5.2).

Logic models help to ensure that project activities are properly aligned to produce the necessary outputs that generate targeted short-term

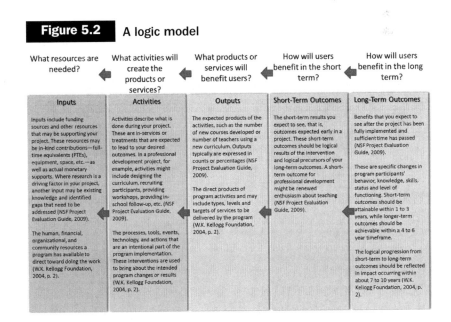

Figure 5.2 A logic model

and long-term benefits to user knowledge, skills and functioning. They serve to formally define the purpose of a project and ensure all members of a project team are on the same page. Most importantly, the logic model can serve as the evaluation plan by identifying specifically what the project's performance objectives are and how it intends on arriving there.

The final step towards creating a logic model is to create a logical progression that links inputs, activities, outputs, short-term outcomes and long-term outcomes. Using our strategic goals from Chapter 2, in Figure 5.3 let us look at what a logic model might look like.

Notice the four strategic goals listed in the strategic plan are in fact considered outputs, or the products and services that lead to short-term and long-term outcomes for the library users, in the logic model. Short-term outcomes resulting in longer-term outcomes for users are identified. In addition, contextual factors are '. . . the specific circumstances that define the locale or situation in which a project is carried out. Potential factors include demographics, state policies, local economic conditions, etc.' (National Science Foundation, 2009) which also inform the overall project environment and logic model flow.

Figure 5.3 Strategic goals logic model

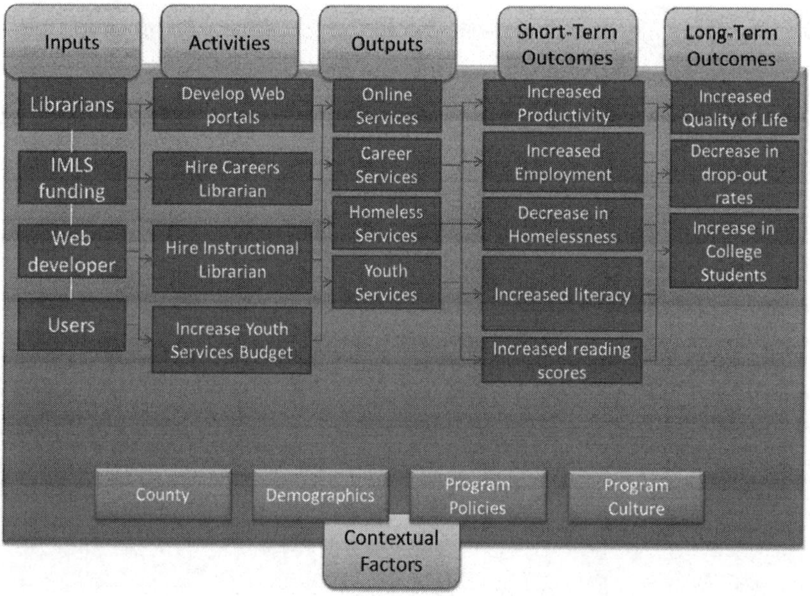

Inputs	Activities	Outputs	Short-Term Outcomes	Long-Term Outcomes
Librarians	Develop Web portals	Online Services	Increased Productivity	Increased Quality of Life
IMLS funding	Hire Careers Librarian	Career Services	Increased Employment	Decrease in drop-out rates
Web developer	Hire Instructional Librarian	Homeless Services	Decrease in Homelessness	Increase in College Students
Users	Increase Youth Services Budget	Youth Services	Increased literacy	
			Increased reading scores	

Contextual Factors: County, Demographics, Program Policies, Program Culture

Once a logic model (also considered an evaluation plan) has been created, the next steps would be to identify evaluation questions around measurable outcomes, develop the evaluation design (National Science Foundation, 2009) and then finally identify data collection methods and data types to be collected. A final data collection table derived directly from the logic model evaluation plan might look something like Table 5.1.

Table 5.1   Logic model data collection

Activities	Goals (outputs)	Data collection method	Data and analysis
1. Develop web portal 2. Content creation	Goal 1: Quality online services (output)	• Collection of documentation • Web analytics • Interviews • Focus Groups	• Hit counts and unique visitors; Frequencies and totals, percentages and means
1. Social networking 2. Digital library 3. Hire career librarian	Goal 2: Quality career services (output)	• Documentation of 'best practices' implemented • Documentation of digital library • Documentation of social network sites, hit counts	• Hit counts and unique visitors; Frequencies and totals, percentages and means
1. Hire instructional librarian 2. Conduct a needs assessment 3. Design homeless services plan	Goal 3: Homeless services (output)	• Collection of documentation • Interviews • Focus Groups	• Users served; median, means and percentages; ANOVA
1. Develop youth services plan 2. Increase youth services funding	Goal 4: Youth services (output)	• Collection of documentation • Interviews • Focus Groups	• Median, means and percentages; ANOVA

6

Emerging technology trends in libraries

Abstract: Where is library technology and automation headed in the next 10 years? This chapter provides an overview of current worldwide technology trends and the implications of these for libraries of today and tomorrow. Current and emerging technologies – such as e-books, e-readers, mobile computing, cloud computing, instructional literacy, and virtual worlds – are discussed. In addition, the concepts of pervasive usability and how to test that your technology is highly efficient, effective, and satisfying for your users are also explained in detail.

Key words: ILS, Web 2.0, e-books, e-readers, mobile technology, digitization, cloud computing, virtual worlds, instructional literacy, usability, usability testing.

The pace of technological change is rapid. At any given time, a host of new library technologies is available and many more are imminent. Of course, no library can afford to implement each and every innovation as soon as it becomes available. Libraries must match new technologies to user and institutional needs, and seek to separate long-term trends from short-term fads.

One consideration in adopting new technologies is the institutional appetite for change. Is your library bleeding edge, cutting edge, or a follower? Each strategy entails its own risks and rewards. It certainly costs more to be an early adopter, but it is sometimes possible to offset those expenses with innovation grants, or by raising the institutional profile regionally, or even nationally. Libraries that choose to 'play it safe' can learn from the mistakes and successes of others, but will never be perceived as leaders. There is no 'best' answer as to how aggressive a library should be in pursuing innovation. What is most important is that each library remains open to appropriate change and that there is an organizational consensus regarding the pace of information technology adoption and implementation. One of the more difficult things to consider before implementing a new technology or product is how it will work in the future. The software and hardware worlds move very quickly and if a library takes six months to assess all their options, then the options may well change significantly over that six-month period – which can make the assessments outdated before they are even completed! When a library buys a product or service they are buying it not only on the basis of what it will do for library users today, but also with the hope that it will grow and change to meet the evolving needs of library users over the next few years. Therefore, technology decisions need to be made with an eye to the future. As a rule of thumb, libraries should be looking three years ahead before making any large-scale technology commitments. The speed of innovation makes it very difficult to make long-term plans beyond that three-year window.

When looking ahead over the next three years, the authors see several important trends that will likely have a significant impact on all types of libraries.

Integrated library systems

An integrated library system (ILS) is a complex program/database that brings multiple library functions together in a (hopefully) seamless manner. The individual functions, usually called 'modules', include such things as:

- the OPAC (or online public access catalog), which is the interface library users use to search the catalog;

- acquisitions module, for keeping track of book orders and expenditures;

- serials module, for keeping track of newspaper and magazine subscriptions and check-in;

- cataloging module, for entering MARC records into the catalog so that items can be found in the OPAC;

- circulation module, to keep track of what is checked out and when it is due back, and to keep up with patron information such as phone numbers, addresses and library cards.

Of the many technological decisions and implementations in libraries, the ILS receives by far the most attention. This is largely because the ILS has typically received the most usage of any library system. But it is also because, unlike most library technology, almost every single library employee interacts with the ILS on a regular basis. In fact, many library employees (particularly in the acquisitions and cataloging departments) spend the majority of their work day using the ILS.

Because an ILS selection can have an enormous impact on the workflow and jobs of most library employees, it is usually the one technological decision that is truly made on a library-wide basis. In a way, it is wonderful that everyone in the library is so interested in, and wants to be involved in, selecting the ILS. But on the other hand, trying to involve everyone is very difficult – especially if they all feel very personally invested in the outcome.

The breadth of involvement in the ILS selection process will probably diminish over the next few years, as the centrality of library catalogs shrinks. When online catalogs first became available in the 1980s, a very high percentage of library patrons used the catalog and everyone using a library computer was searching the catalog. Today, the catalog continues to play an important role, but competes with many other information resources in high demand by our users (e-mail, web, databases, e-books, etc.). In the future, the catalog will probably be searched less and less often as a stand-alone database and will instead be searched more often in conjunction with other information resources.

The current library paradigm divides information into many different silos, each of which must be searched independently by users. If someone wants a physical book that the library owns, they should search the library catalog. If they want an article, they should search an article database. If they want an older e-book, they should search Google Books. Librarians may enjoy mastering this complex and bifurcated information environment, but library users do not. When faced with an array of search options and locations, the invariable response is, 'Why can't this be a single search box, like Google?'

Library ILSs have been information silos in another sense, too. For the most part, each library runs its own ILS locally on its own hardware. These ILSs contain MARC records that are very similar to records in other ILSs. In other words, multiple libraries with copies of the same book are likely each maintaining identical (or very similar) library catalog records for that item. Looked at across the entire profession, this model involves a high degree of duplication of effort for both records and hardware maintenance. In the current climate of budget cuts and austerity, it seems likely that libraries will move away from the local ILS model and will instead share a cloud-based library catalog. At the cost of some local control and ability to customize, libraries should be able to more cost-effectively share a single catalog and a single copy of each MARC record. This model of resource sharing fits well with librarians' strong record of sharing through such vehicles as OCLC and interlibrary loan.

The only product currently in development that will allow libraries to truly share data and hardware on a global scale is OCLC's WorldCat Web-Scale Management Services. At the time of this writing, it is too early to declare OCLC's efforts a complete success, but they are clearly on the right strategic path. If, for any reason, OCLC Web-Scale fails to live up to its potential, it seems highly likely that another cloud-based ILS will emerge and allow broad resource sharing and enormous collective cost savings across all library types. Within the next three years, we will see significant movement away from the local ILS and towards a shared, cloud-based ILS.

Metasearching and discovery tools

Metasearching (also known as federated searching) is the ability to simultaneously search multiple resources. For example, from a single search box, a library user could with a single click search the library catalog, other nearby library catalogs, the web, the library's website, subscription databases (such as InfoTrac) and locally developed materials such as an archive of digitized local history documents.

The value to the user is obvious. Instead of having to conduct numerous searches, each using their own unique search syntax, the user can easily and quickly retrieve a single, combined search response list in relevance order. Or at least, that was the promise of federated searching. The technology never achieved its full promise because, instead of fixing the fundamental problems of searching multiple resources, it merely masked them. When a user entered a search term and hit the 'Enter' key, the products still launched simultaneous searches against all of the resource targets (catalogs, databases, e-book collections, etc.) and then tried to make sense of the results as the various systems responded. As one might expect, the results of this shotgun approach to searching were slow and inconsistent.

Recently, a new breed of 'single search box' tools has been released. Known as 'discovery tools', these products aggregate different resource types from different locations into a single database and then allow that single database to be readily searched from one box. Although this technology is still new, it is clear that discovery tools offer significant advantages over their predecessors. Currently available commercial products include EBSCO Discovery Service, Summon and Primo Central. These cloud-based services combine proprietary commercial data (such as articles from subscription journals and magazines) with locally controlled data from the library catalog, institutional repository, or other system. The result is a seamless, single search interface for all data types.

Some libraries, primarily academic, host their own local implementation of a discovery tool that aggregates disparate data types. But because single institutions don't have the clout to convince commercial publishers to share proprietary data, such local discovery tools generally allow the searching of only the library catalog and a few other locally controlled or produced data sets. Some examples in this category include VuFind, Blacklight and Endeca. Within the next three years, large numbers of libraries will feature a single search box on their home page. Information silos such as the library catalog may still exist, but will be relegated to a less prominent position within a library's website.

Web 2.0

The terms 'Web 2.0' and 'Library 2.0' are a bit nebulous, but are generally considered to include a user-centered approach and a high degree of interactivity, usually in a technology-driven, multimedia environment. Although the concept of Web 2.0 is sound, we feel it hasn't always been implemented very thoughtfully in most libraries (particularly in academic libraries). For example, one of the core drivers of Library 2.0 is the assumption that because many of today's library patrons are avid users of social networking services (Flickr, YouTube, Twitter, MySpace, Facebook, etc.), there is consequently a heavy demand for a strong library presence via these media. But that may or may not be a valid leap of logic. Although some users may appreciate a library's entrance into social networking, other users tend to resent, rather than welcome, libraries' attempts to engage them on social sites. Most usage data reports very low usage of library services delivered via social media, even while more and more libraries rush to implement them.

Part of the issue relates to scale. Amazon, with its hundreds of millions of customers, has achieved the requisite critical mass for audience interaction such as user-provided book reviews. But a small public library with a fraction of that user base would be less likely to see user-driven content succeed in the same way. Of course, if we all end up sharing a single, cloud-based ILS, then that will enable us to aggregate library users and achieve the critical mass necessary for many Web 2.0 services. Over the next three years, libraries will continue to invest in experimenting with Web 2.0 to see what works and what does not. And that's particularly apt for Web 2.0, because one of its underlying principles is continuous improvement and the idea that it is okay to be in perpetual beta mode.

E-books and e-readers

Many people who read have a strong preference for the physical, printed artifact and are ambivalent or negative about the digital version. That's partly because books are cheap and easy on the eyes over long periods. But much of our connection to physical books is a cultural one. Books have long symbolized learning and are seen as the medium by which ancestral knowledge descended to the present day.

Of course, e-books have many distinct advantages over printed materials, such as:

- ability to change font and font size;
- a whole library available at once;
- potential hyperlinking to related materials and to reference materials such as dictionaries, encyclopedias and websites;
- no need for bookmarks;
- internal light source (for when you are trying to read and your partner wants to sleep);
- potential of lower cost per book;
- keyword searchable;
- can cut and paste.

But despite these advantages, over the past decade e-books have just not caught on to the same extent that e-journals have. We believe that is mainly because we have a cultural connection to the book that we just don't have with journals.

Today, e-books stand poised to enter the mainstream and truly compete with their printed counterparts. On 26 December 2009, an Amazon press release stated 'On Christmas Day, for the first time ever, customers purchased more Kindle books than physical books' (Amazon, 2009). US sales data from 2009 reveal a 176.6 percent increase in e-book sales, compared to a much more modest 1.8 percent increase for printed books (Association of American Publishers, 2010). And the *New York Times* announced that their venerable best-seller lists would begin including e-books as a separate category in 2011 (Bosman, 2010).

Much of the new interest in e-books is driven by the latest generation of e-book readers, the best known of which are the Kindle, Nook, Sony Reader and iPad. These products offer enough features and benefits to tempt even the most ardent bibliophiles. Unfortunately, these items are designed more for personal use than for libraries, which causes some logistical issues in a library setting. For example, most Kindle books are subject to a five-device limit. So, if a library ordered 1,000 Kindle books and wanted to check them all out to users via 20 Kindle devices, it would be very difficult because any given book would be available via only five of the physical Kindles. A library could potentially have many Kindles available for circulation, but not have one that held the specific book the patron wanted to read.

Despite the limitations of the readers, many libraries are moving aggressively into the e-book world. One reason is budgetary. E-books are typically cheaper to purchase and are less expensive to house and maintain. Some studies suggest they also see higher usage levels than the same title in print (Littman and Connaway, 2004).

E-books offer libraries the opportunity to radically redefine collection development and move from a just-in-case inventory model to a just-in-time delivery model. Traditionally, librarians have selected and purchased specific books in anticipation of their use. We would then house those books until a user needed them. With e-books, we can go a different route. Through services such as Rittenhouse's R2 and Coutts' MyiLibrary, a library can load into their catalog the bibliographic records for a large numbers of e-books. Library patrons can search, retrieve and read these e-books. Once the book has been read a certain number of times, the library is charged for the title. Thus, purchase follows usage, rather than the other way around. Early feedback on this innovative approach strongly suggests that it leads to higher usage levels than the traditional collection development model.

As of early 2011, Google has digitized roughly 12 million books, including about 2 million in the public domain (most of which were published prior to 1923). The complete full text of the 2 million is readily and freely available, but only snippets and excerpts are available for the rest. At the time of this writing, it seems more likely than not that in the next few years the Google Books Settlement will be accepted and implemented. If it is, the number of publicly available full text e-books will increase dramatically – perhaps to the point where Google becomes the repository for nearly all printed works.

Google has promised that they will provide each library one Google access station at no cost, which can be used by patrons to access this vast electronic library. But libraries will have to pay if they want more such stations. If people can access nearly any book on Google, that fact will no doubt have a significant impact on the range and number of books that a library collects either in print or online.

Google Books will also have a profound impact on the library catalog. For centuries, library users have searched a card catalog or ILS that contains brief bibliographic information on a title; they have not been able to search the full text of the library's holdings. But because Google Books has the digitized the full text of the collections of Harvard, Cornell, Michigan and other pre-eminent libraries, they are highly likely to have the full text of nearly any book in any given public or academic library. So, in effect, Google Books will allow full text searching of most libraries, rendering the current bibliographic library catalog largely obsolete.

For those readers who still prefer the printed book to the online version, print-on-demand will provide rapid and cost-effective printing of e-books. Machines such as On Demand Books' Espresso can print and bind in seven minutes a 300-page paperback book that is comparable to those purchased in bookstores. It is not farfetched to consider that tomorrow's libraries may never purchase just-in-case books again. They could simply print-on-demand as titles are requested and then house those copies on their shelves.

An overwhelming number of users equate libraries with 'books' (De Rosa et al., 2005). It will be very interesting to see if that perception changes as e-books explode and begin to truly supplant (rather than simply supplement) the large printed book collections in most libraries. Over the next few years, Google Books, full text searchability, patron-driven book selection, enhanced e-readers and print-on-demand services will radically transform libraries.

Pay per view

Pay per view (PPV) offers another demand-driven and cost-effective approach to collection management in the twenty-first century. It is particularly well suited to seldom-used items and to portions of an entire work (e.g. chapters of a book, or an article from a journal). With PPV, a library incurs a charge each time an item is read. The library can typically place cost ceilings or other limits on these charges to ensure that the service stays within its budget. Aggregators such as Ingenta offer PPV for a wide variety of publishers, while individual publishers such as Wiley and Elsevier offer their own journals and book chapters via PPV. Typical costs for an article range from \$20 to \$40. While this may seem quite expensive, depending on the frequency of use, PPV can be much cheaper than journal subscriptions costing many thousands of dollars.

Because serials inflation has been the fastest growing portion of collections budgets, many libraries will seek to contain their subscription costs in response to increased budgetary pressures. As a viable alternative for providing access to seldom-used materials, PPV will be offered more widely (particularly in academic libraries) over the next few years.

Consortia and group purchasing

Librarians tend to view one another more as colleagues than as competitors. We have learned that, by acting collectively, we can more effectively promote and spread our professional values of literacy, learning and preserving knowledge. As new technologies became available, such services as interlibrary loan and OCLC shared cataloging extended that cooperation to virtually every library.

Today's shrinking budgets are likely to place even more emphasis on resource sharing through consortia. For example, individual libraries may be reluctantly forced to cancel resources or services due to local budgetary limitations. But while the library may not be able to fully fund the program on its own, it may be able to continue it by cost-sharing with equally cash-strapped libraries. When libraries join together, the total cost can be split across several budgets, reducing the participation expense for each individual library.

Library resource consortia or 'buyer's clubs' are particularly effective examples of leveraging scarce resources for the greater good. Many groups have centralized the negotiation, purchase and management of e-resources and services on behalf of multiple libraries. In the US, one of the best known examples is OhioLINK, which provides a library catalog, over 150 research databases and over 10,000 e-journals to 88 college and university libraries at a fraction of what it would cost the constituent members to purchase comparable services on their own.

Most libraries participate in some sort of centrally-funded resource consortium, but many also participate in self-funded 'buyer's clubs' that allow each library to opt in or out of any particular group deal. One example is the Carolina Consortium, a group of over 130 libraries in North and South Carolina. Although the consortium has negotiated over 75 group deals, no library participates in more than half of them and many join only a handful of deals. Nevertheless, the aggregate savings are significant. The group estimates that through the power of bulk purchasing the group is paying approximately $250 million less than if each library purchased the same resources independently (Carolina Consortium, n.d.).

For decades, libraries have derived significant value through collective action and economies of scale. As local budgets shrink, libraries will turn to consortiums and group purchasing to get the best possible return on each dollar spent.

Media

Libraries of all types are circulating a wider array of media, with movies being among the most popular with both libraries and their customers. At this time, DVDs are the primary format for circulating movies. Faced with growing demand, some libraries have turned to video vending machines to house and distribute their media collections. The Princeton Public Library was among the first to host a Red Box of the same type found in many grocery stores (Hermann, 2008). Recently, products such as 3M's Library Media Box have been designed specifically for the library market. It is too early to say if these products will take off, but libraries will continue to look for new models to meet the public's growing demand for media.

Some libraries are experimenting with streaming media as an alternative method of delivering videos to patrons. Although licensing issues prevent libraries from legally offering a centralized Netflix service, there are some companies that are willing to work with libraries. Some of these, such as Films on Demand or Alexander Street Press's Ethnographic Videos Online, offer niche films. Others, including Swank Digital Media, offer more first-run and popular films in their catalog.

Over the next few years, the circulation of media will continue to grow and will become a greater percentage of overall library collection usage. In the short term, media vending machines may help libraries accommodate this growth. But soon libraries will turn to streaming media as a more cost-effective and scalable solution for delivering movies to their patrons.

Meeting spaces

Traditionally, libraries were designed as places where users could quietly interact with books or other materials. That function is still important, but today there is an increasing focus on encouraging and enabling users to interact with one another and with librarians. This expanded activity takes place in many spaces within libraries and often occurs face to face, without significant technological intervention, in cafés, meeting rooms, clustered work tables, theatres, or group studies.

But many of the library's group spaces do have a strong technological orientation. These technology-enhanced group spaces go by many names – collaboratories, learning commons, information commons, etc. They may have differing designs, software and equipment, but they often have similar goals – to expand the traditional role of the library and to potentially bring a new group of users into the building. Given the high usage rates and enthusiastic reception by the user community at most libraries, we seem to be fairly successful in providing the technology and physical environment for collaborative spaces.

The University of North Carolina at Greensboro (UNCG) provides examples of several types of collaborative spaces, each configured to meet the needs of a different group. UNCG's Information Commons has a variety of table configurations, each with a PC that can be used by a group. This wireless-enabled area is located near a high-traffic zone within the Library and is available on a first-come, first-served basis. It is highly popular with students who form spontaneous groups and with groups that will be meeting for a relatively short period.

For groups in need of quiet, more focused research space, the library offers two types of collaboratories. There are seven of the smaller rooms, each of which seat four people and provide a networked PC, a 36-inch plasma screen, whiteboards and wireless access. The library also has two larger collaboratories, each with a networked PC, 50-inch plasma screen, whiteboards, wireless and a podium for presentation practice. The collaboratories can be reserved online and are quite heavily used.

Other libraries are using cutting-edge technologies to offer innovative new capabilities and services to groups. For example, the North Carolina State University Libraries are constructing a 'Technology Sandbox' that will provide gesture-based interactions with visualized data on screens that span an entire wall. Using technologies more usually available only to large television news organizations, students and faculty will be able to use a technology-rich learning space that blends the physical and the virtual.

Providing physical space for groups is not the only way for libraries to become more actively involved in collaborative discussions. Instead of offering new services to groups in our space (our library building), we can reach out to their space instead. And increasingly, that space is virtual. In an academic environment, a Course Management System (such as Blackboard, WebCT, Sakai, or Moodle) offers opportunities for librarians to embed themselves in group discussions and assist with research. Other venues, such as blogs or Facebook, provide alternative avenues for contacting or working with academic or public library users.

These online venues often allow libraries to offer services directed at a particular segment of their audience. For example, a public librarian could sponsor or participate in a real-time online discussion group of Agatha Christie mysteries. Because all participants are self selected as interested in this topic, this online group would be a great place to mention the library's new online exhibition of Christie letters. Even more customization is possible in any environment that requires login. For example, at the University of North Carolina at Greensboro, the library constructed a web service that interfaces with the campus' online course management system (Blackboard) and presents users with the relevant library resources, based on their status, major, minor and currently enrolled courses. So, an undergraduate psychology major logging into Blackboard would see a different list of library journals, databases and online reserves than an English professor would see.

Over the next few years, libraries of all types will place a greater emphasis on group and collaborative spaces. These spaces will become more likely to include significant information technology components. Libraries will also become more active in virtual spaces and will use them to create more individually customized user experiences.

Circulating devices

Libraries of all types have successfully embraced the circulation of a range of devices, including digital cameras, flash drives, laptops, e-readers, MP3 players and more. As the public appetite for these technologies grows, it seems likely that circulating services will continue to expand over the next few years. Public libraries will need to balance the increased need for circulating devices with the also-increasing need for circulating traditional materials. In academic libraries, we could see a major shift in circulation emphasis as traditional collection check-outs continue to decline and device circulation increases rapidly. School libraries may see some increase in device circulation, but it will be limited by the fact that in most cases these services can only be offered to teachers and some older students. Overall, we will see a great increase in the types and volume of device circulation in libraries. And that is entirely appropriate; the role of the library in providing egalitarian access to both information and information technology is well established and should be applied to new technologies as they become available.

Mobile

We are a mobile society. More than 80 percent of Americans have cell phones and 59 percent use a laptop or cell phone to access the Internet (Smith, 2010). Libraries must effectively present their online services to this enormous mobile audience, but doing so presents significant challenges.

Different types of cell phones have different capabilities, which means that libraries must choose between customizing services for a wide range of phones, or offering services only to some types of phones and not others. And even when we succeed in making our own services mobile-friendly, we still face issues in connecting our mobile users to third-party content. For example, a library can make its online database page work well on mobile devices, but when a user actually selects a database they will leave the library site and go to a vendor site that may or may not be usable through mobile devices.

One of the most exciting opportunities for library mobile applications relates to geolocation. Many smart phones (e.g. iPhone, some Android phones, etc.) have built in GPS, so the phone knows exactly where it is. Libraries can use this feature to give their users information related to their current physical location. For example, a library could digitize its collection of historical photos of downtown. Citizens driving or strolling down Main Street could then use their mobile device to see how specific buildings or locations looked many years ago.

Quick Response (QR) codes are another mobile application with potential for libraries. These matrix barcodes can be posted virtually anywhere. A user with a camera-equipped phone can take a picture of the QR code and use an application such as BeeTagg or RedLaser to trigger an event. For example, a library could post a QR code near the door of the library and deliver the library's home page and hours to anyone scanning that code. Or a library could post QR codes over its current print journals, which would then send interested users to the electronic version of that publication.

Mobile support will become increasingly important to libraries over the next few years. Because mobile services have a large technology component, this could well push the entire profession towards a more technology-oriented skill set for librarians.

Digitization

The storing, organizing and lending of published materials is a major focus at most libraries. While this role will remain important, it will diminish somewhat as pay-per-view, print-on-demand, the transition to e-books and massive digitization projects make it quicker and more convenient for users to interact with published materials without using the library as an intermediary. To some, this might seem a signal of the imminent death of librarianship. Can libraries survive as increasing numbers of their users begin to get their books elsewhere?

One possible response is for libraries to reposition themselves. Rather than acting as an intermediary between a book's publisher and its audience, libraries can become content creators. Most academic libraries have special collections that are veritable treasure troves of valuable, but unpublished and inaccessible materials. Public libraries have special collections, genealogy rooms and a clear stake in preserving and disseminating the history and culture of the community they serve. Libraries of all types can identify under-utilized, unpublished materials and scan or otherwise digitize them and make them available on the Internet. The possibilities are almost limitless: audio of oral histories of local residents, early photographs, manuscripts, letters – or combine them all to create an interactive community map with embedded multimedia.

Such efforts can provide many benefits for a participating library. Many grants are available, so a digitization program could potentially be self-sustaining. Opportunities abound for community engagement. Also, rather than simply housing copies of published books that other libraries also have, the library contributes its own unique materials to the global knowledge pool and shares them world-wide. Making as many worthy materials as possible, and as broadly available as possible, is one of the primary values of librarianship and it is one that will be emphasized through enhanced digitization programs over the next few years.

Cloud computing

Today, most libraries maintain local servers that run local applications such as the library catalog. This arrangement requires significant initial outlay in establishing a professional grade server operation within the library. It also requires significant ongoing costs in terms of staffing, training and hardware replacement. Running local servers does give libraries the maximum amount of control over their computing infrastructure and environment, but it can also be quite expensive.

As budgets continue to tighten, libraries are increasingly considering moving more operations to cloud computing environments. In such a model, many libraries share a pool of computing resources that are accessible over the network. Because the cost is shared widely, the cost per institution can be lower. Additional savings are gained through efficiencies. For example, if a local ILS server is typically used at only half its capacity and only rarely achieves high CPU utilization, then half of its computing cycles are being wasted. But in a cloud environment, that spare computing power can be used by another application or user.

Pooling and sharing resources is something libraries have always done to some extent (for example, we have a long history of loaning our books to one another). There is little doubt that we will extend that concept to the library's computing hardware and that the library systems of the future will be hosted in the cloud.

Pervasive web usability and usability testing

Libraries and librarians have considerable expertise in connecting users to the information they need. A couple of decades ago, a library's reference desk had been the key intermediation point between users and information. While the reference desk continues to play a vital role, many users have today opted to begin their searching online. In effect, our web pages have now subsumed much of the traditional reference role of guiding people to appropriate information resources. Because the web has become a key (and perhaps primary) point of contact between the library and its users, it is critical that we have an effective and usable web presence.

Web designers must contend with a number of unique variables. The first main variable is platform and browser compatibility. Mozilla Firefox is by a wide margin the most popular browser, followed by Internet Explorer and Google Chrome. All three, however, represent unique software applications that read and interact with web pages somewhat differently. A given web page viewed through Firefox will not necessarily look exactly the same as the same page viewed through Chrome. And a web page viewed through an older version of Firefox may not look the same as it would when viewed by the most recent Firefox. Similarly, computers with different operating systems may interact differently with web pages and web applications. In addition, the continued emergence of tablet PCs, smart phones and other wireless devices must be taken into account by web designers.

The second main design variable is the connection speed of users. While broadband continues to grow in the United States, over 25 percent of the US population still has limited or no Internet connectivity at all from their home. The third variable is the use of multimedia on the web. This combines the first and second factors because each will largely determine the quality of the user's multimedia experience. The extent of usage of multimedia on a website is largely dependent on the expected technology capabilities of an information organization's typical user.

The concept of *pervasive usability* is critical for ensuring the overall efficiency and effectiveness of Internet delivered content and can be defined as a process that '. . . advocates the application of methods to evaluate a design's usability at every stage of the design process, keeping in mind the goals of the project and the users' needs' (Kheterpal, 2003). An applied model for implementing pervasive usability throughout the design and development cycle is the Design, Development and Evaluation (DDE) model (Chow, 2011).

The *design* phase involves identifying preliminary user requirements, thus establishing a feature checklist or list of required features in priority order, which then leads to an initial site information architecture. As they are developed, the identified requirements, feature checklist and information architecture should be vetted with representative users and refined accordingly. The site only needs to exist on paper, storyboard, or basic HTML at this first stage.

The second stage is *develop*, which now involves the initial development of a user interface specifying color, layout, and use of graphics and multimedia. The development stage will involve alpha, beta and final implementation versions of the site with each undergoing iterative usability tests focused on users' abilities to effectively perform the primary tasks identified in the design stage.

The final stage is the *evaluate* stage, where the released website is again formally usability tested, which begins the entire DDE pervasive usability cycle again and ensures the long-term, consistent continuous improvement of the website (Figure 6.1).

The most scientifically valid way to measure the effectiveness of a website is through usability testing. There are two types of usability testing: empirical (with users) and non-empirical (without users) (Jordan, 2001).

Empirical usability testing involves:

- Conducting user surveys, interviews and focus groups which help identify and establish user requirements.
- User testing:
  - task analysis where users attempt to complete actual tasks developed around the website's identified feature checklist;
  - collection of usability metrics: time, error rate and user satisfaction (frequently recorded);
  - think-aloud protocols: testers articulate their thought processes while attempting to complete tasks;
  - natural observations;
  - user debriefings through interviews, surveys and focus groups.

Figure 6.1 The design, develop and evaluate pervasive usability model

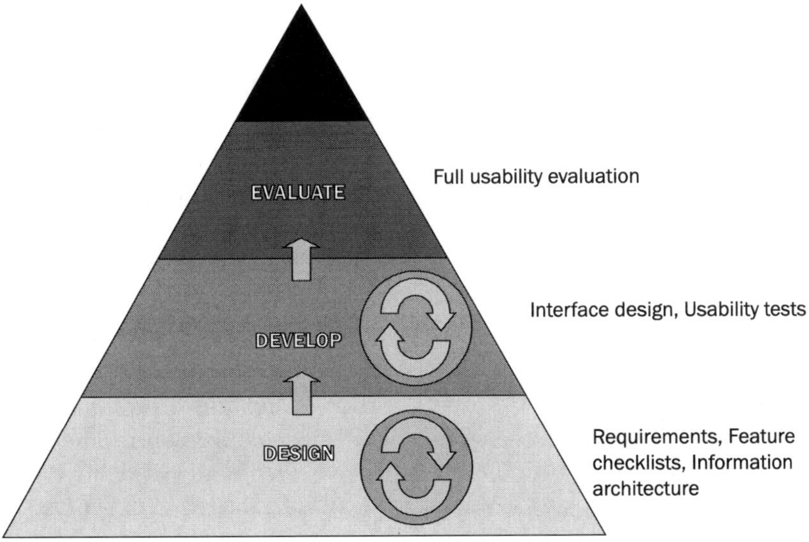

Non-empirical testing involves:

- *Examination of web analytics*: Web statistics are examined for user and site trends.
- *Cognitive walkthroughs*: Usability evaluator walks through the website trying to complete main site tasks looking for potential problems involving high levels of cognitive effort.
- *Heuristic or usability standard evaluation*: Website is compared to established usability heuristics.

Another major website usability variable is the median age of its primary user community. There is a growing body of literature suggesting that the information seeking behaviour of adults, teenage young adults (14–18) and middle-school-age youth (12–14) is significantly different. Adults are typically more likely to seek specific information and often '. . . ignore features such as navigation bars, animation and sound effects and rarely pay attention to logos, mission statements, or advertising within a website' (Neilson, 2005; Chow et al., 2011). They prefer quick downloads, consistency and predictability, text-based links and broad, shallow, tree structures for information architecture (Lazar, 2003 as cited in Chow et al., 2011).

High-school-aged information seekers (14–18) prefer easy-to-use sites with clean designs and 'cool' graphics; they also like interacting through online quizzes, voting and games, and participating in sharing activities, such as forums, message boards and Wikis. This group is also particularly resistant to any visual designs perceived as 'child'-focused, including childish content, images, or color schemes (Nielsen, 2005; Chow et al., 2011). They also like vivid photographs (DiMichele, 2007) and tend to use visual cues while ignoring distractions such as scrolling text or moving images (Fidel et al., 1999).

Middle-school students (12–14) tend to prefer specific visual cues with bright and engaging colors along with animation and sound effects (Nielsen, 2005) to capture their attention and keep them engaged (Large et al., 2002). They also tend to like the use of icons and mascots, interesting website names and prefer browsing as opposed to searching (Large et al., 2006).

Understanding basic preferences for youth, however, is not enough. In our work with designing STEM career websites for middle-school and high-school students for the NSF-funded STARS Alliance project (*www .starsallliance.org*), we found that it is critical to effectively engage the age group of your primary audience. If an adult paradigm is used to attempt to define what is 'cool' or 'engaging' for a youth age group, a disconnect will occur and the web-based service will likely fail. Indeed, this frequently happens with many websites even if user or focus groups are held, because often the groups are comprised solely of developers, designers, or other technologically inclined users (Lin, 2007). The best way to prevent this from happening and to maintain your website's focus on a youth audience is to make them part of the design team from the very beginning (Druin et al., 1999).

Utilizing representative users as design partners for age-appropriate websites is termed *concept actualization* and is intended 'to authentically embrace and implement a concept in site design through the lens of the users who will be utilizing the site' (Chow et al., 2010: 15). Based on our STEM research we revised the EDDE model (Table 6.1) to incorporate the need for engaging youth as design partners.

Table 6.1 EDDE youth website design model

Phase 1: ENGAGE . . .	
1. Design partners	Put together a small group of age-appropriate users as your design partners
2. Age-appropriate user group	Keep group together so you can seek constant and consistent advice on design standards, specifications and general perceptions and opinions
3. Web designers and developers	Ensure web designers and developers are meeting directly with your youth design partners; seek concept actualization
Phase 2: DESIGN . . .	
4. Site specifications	List main goals of site in priority order
5. Information architecture	Create information architecture map detailing main channels and sub pages
6. User interface on paper	Establish general design elements of color, format, layout, etc.
7. Usability test	Show design to youth design partners; test information architecture through scenario and task completion
8. Refinement	Refine site based on user feedback and usability testing
9. Usability test	Seek user feedback on refinements made (formal testing not necessary)

(Continued overleaf)

Table 6.1 EDDE youth website design model *(cont'd)*

Phase 3: DEVELOP . . .	
10. Alpha version of the site	Using HTML, XHTML, web design software, etc.; develop web pages with images, animations, color, information, hyperlinks, selected functionality, etc.
11. Usability test	Show initial version to design partners; test information architecture and all design and functional elements through scenario and task completion
12. Beta version of the site	Incorporate results of testing into refined version
13. Usability test	Show refined version to design partners; test information architecture and all design and functional elements through scenario and task completion
14. Usability test final beta version	Seek user feedback on refinements made (formal testing not necessary)
15. Version 1.0 and release to public	After making final refinements roll site live (note: certainly another iteration of design and usability testing can occur)
Phase 4: EVALUATE . . .	
16. By collecting user feedback informally	Informally collect user feedback by utilizing an online survey and/or user feedback/comment box that is available anytime
17. Through formal usability testing	Conduct usability test by engaging age-appropriate users that are not design partners; test information architecture and all design and functional elements through scenario and task completion
18. Results to refine site accordingly leading to start of second Engagement phase.	Utilizing results begins refinement and starts the design and development of a second version of your site; this begins the entire EDDE process again.

While full scale usability tests might seem complex and intimidating, they can be conducted fairly simply and inexpensively. Tests typically involve only five to seven users and do not require any expensive hardware (although higher-end labs do have specialized software like Morae and even eyeball tracking hardware). Given the relatively low cost and the critical importance of our web interfaces, we believe that the expansion of usability testing offers significant opportunities to libraries of all types. Libraries could even choose to offer usability testing services to their parent organizations. An academic library could test the pages of the university or the pages of academic departments. The public library could test and analyze the efficacy of the web presence of the local government. Increased emphasis on usability testing could help reinforce and extend into the future the library's traditional expertise as intermediary between the user and the information they are seeking.

Over the next few years, we hope to see usability testing begin to play a much more prominent role in libraries.

Virtual worlds

A virtual world is a simulated environment, accessed by multiple users through an online interface. Virtual users can then interact with these worlds using unique, customizable avatars that are virtual representations of themselves. In 2007, Gartner Chief of Research, Steve Prentice, boldly predicted that by 2011 there would be 50–60 million users. He stated: 'They're my kids, to be honest, back from school, right onto MySpace', and that the projection was meant as 'a wake-up call to the CIO and CEOS out there that this is not a game, just sort of messing around. It's interesting [and] we think it's going to be big' (Wagner, 2007). This bold prediction, however, was off . . . way off. In October 2010 there were over 1 billion registered virtual users worldwide with over half of them 15 years of age or younger (Watters, 2010).

The overwhelming majority of these users are aged 25 years or younger; 468 million of these user accounts are registered to users between the ages of 10 and 15 years, and another 288 million accounts are registered to users aged 15 to 25 years (ibid.). According to *Forbes* magazine as of 2007, the most popular virtual worlds include Active Worlds, Club Penguin and Runescape (Schifrin, 2007):

Virtual world	Web address
Active Worlds (1997)	*http://www.activeworlds.com/*
BarbieGirls (2007)	*http://www.barbiegirls.com/*
Club Penguin (2006)	*http://www.clubpenguin.com/*
Gaia Online (2003)	*http://www.gaiaonline.com/*

Habbo Hotel (2001)	*http://www.habbo.com/*
RuneScape (2001)	*http://www.runescape.com/*
Second Life (2003)	*http://secondlife.com/*
The Sims Online (2002)	*http://thesims.ea.com/*
Webkinz (2005)	*http://www.webkinz.com/*
World of Warcraft (2004)	*http://us.battle.net/wow*

While there were 85 virtual worlds in 2008, that number grew to 150 by 2009, to approximately 300 by 2010 and was projected to exceed 500 by 2011 (KZero Worldswide, 2011). For the under-15 age group, Stardoll (*http://www.stardoll.com*) is one of the most popular sites with 69 million registered users, while Habbo (*http://www.habbo.com/*) is the largest with 150 million registered users (Watters, 2010). In terms of absolute numbers, there are 'four sweet-spots' that make up large majorities of virtual registered users aged under 25 years: 9-year-olds (over 70 million), 11-year-olds (over 50 million), 14-year-olds (approximately 200 million) and 19-year-olds (over 30 million). Ninety-seven percent of all virtual accounts belong to people aged 25 years or younger, with 10–15-year-olds representing 46 percent of all registered virtual users, followed by 15–25-year-olds at 29 percent, 5 to 10-year-olds at 22 percent and 25+ year olds representing just 3 percent (Figure 6.2) (KZero Worldswide, 2011).

Figure 6.2 Breakdown of virtual users

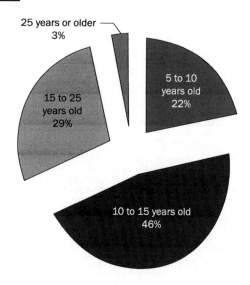

Virtual worlds are the realm of the young. What should libraries make of this? According to Peters (2008: 5), virtual worlds today are either 'negatively dismissive or alluringly positive', and they are consequently seen as a waste of time by some and an exciting breath of fresh air by others. Interest in virtual worlds for libraries remains an emerging area with over 120 virtual libraries existing in Second Life as of 2007 (Kroski, 2007). We conducted a case study with some of our students of one public library's journey, the Olathe (Kansas) public library, into the virtual world Second Life and found mixed success. The initiative has been led by Lorie Hyten, a librarian with tremendous vision who is seeking the opportunity for librarians to become technology leaders rather than simply followers. Our research, however, found limited support at the library and a lack of clear goals for service provision through Olathe's virtual library branch. In a survey of 56 users of Olathe's bricks-and-mortar library, 47 percent of the patrons said they would be interested in a virtual extension of the library while 53 percent said they would not be. Fifty-four percent also said they would be interested in attending a class on Olathe's Second Life library (Chow et al., 2011). In Second Life, we surveyed 285 users and found that 69 percent had used Second Life for less than a month and 80 percent were first-time library visitors. Furthermore, general interest in the library and its resources appeared to be rather exploratory: 79.0 percent never talked with a librarian at the library they visited; 75.3 percent did not come to the library looking for a specific resource; and 68.5 percent did not use any resources while they were visiting the library.

An interview with four Second Life librarians helped illuminate the primary purpose of Second Life virtual libraries: the librarians valued the ability to learn from and work with other library and information professionals all over the world; with an emphasis on the opportunities to learn, network and collaborate across geographical borders in ways that would not be possible without the Internet. They all reported that they could only put in an hour or so per week of actual on-the-clock work time, though the virtual library is sponsored by their employers. They spent many more hours of their own personal time working on and in the Second Life libraries, mainly because they personally felt that the libraries were of great value, essentially making them volunteers (ibid.).

All of the librarians interviewed reiterated the opportunities created for networking and collaboration between libraries that are geographically distant. Most saw Second Life continuing to move in an education-based direction, with possible increasing participation from government entities and businesses. The 3-D environment lends itself particularly well to learning demonstrations. Our conclusion was that virtual libraries serve a different user base – more tech-savvy, more global and less local, with a greater emphasis on education, communication and social networking. Libraries interested in virtual branch libraries should try to avoid duplicating real-life services and instead think of innovative ways to use Second Life's interface to deliver information and services, especially within an educational, networking, or social context.

Little research has been done on how to leverage the fact that the majority of virtual users are youth aged 5 to 15 years, which we project will be an emerging area in library services in the coming years. The children of one of the authors, however, helped fill in the gaps from their perspective. First, users in this age group have multiple accounts, so the statistics showing total number of user accounts is inflated in terms of number of actual, unduplicated users. Between three children, they held almost 40 different accounts across six different virtual worlds. Second, based on their perspective, the main reason why they like playing in virtual worlds, in priority order, is the social interaction and engagement they get with others. Additional reasons include the ability to customize their characters, the ability to do things (like fighting), and play games they cannot do in reality, the fact that it is free and the ability to develop their characters and have a direct impact on how they mature and grow (Chow et al., 2011).

Instructional literacy and technology

> Librarians are educators by default. From the quickest reference interaction to the most in-depth information-literacy initiative or staff-training program, librarians and library staff teach, train, present and design learning materials in every aspect of our jobs, all the time. (Booth, 2010)

The need for providing instruction in libraries to users is almost as pervasive as technology itself. In fact, 41 percent, or 61 million, of those who visited the US's public libraries in 2009, noted the top reason why they visited was for educational purposes – to do homework or take a class (ALA, 2010). Overall, 80 percent of all public libraries offered homework support and classes, and 53 percent reported consistent 'point-of-use assistance' for users with technology. In academic libraries, teaching information literacy to faculty and students is the most commonly cited metric used for validating their strategic value to universities and colleges across the country. School librarians report spending more and more of their time in an instructional role. As this trend continues, librarians and information professionals will need to be prepared to teach a wide variety of users in equally diverse instructional, teaching and learning environments. But in spite of this strong and growing need very few librarians outside of school libraries ever receive formal training or education in how to teach or provide training.

Instructional literacy can be defined as the set of knowledge, skills, attitudes and abilities that must be imparted to users/learners so that increased learning takes place. Booth (2010) has created a four part instructional literacy framework comprised of *reflective practice* (shaping your own skills and abilities), *educational theory* (developing an evidence-based teaching and learning pedagogy), *teaching technologies* (tools and information communication technologies (ICTs) available for teaching and learning) and *instructional design* (a systematic process for delivering teaching and learning) (ibid.).

Building your own instructional literacy foundation involves a diverse set of formal courses, workshops, presentations and hands-on practice and experimentation. Most importantly, it reflects an ever-growing core function of serving users in library and information organizational settings and goes back to the bottom line of libraries in general – meeting the needs of their users. The traditional instructional design model, ADDIE (Analyze, Design, Develop, Implement and Evaluate), is a good general rule of thumb to follow in more formal teaching and learning environments. The AIR (or Analyze, Implement and Resolve) model is better suited for technical support and for one-on-one transactions where the user is seeking help accomplishing an immediate task. Finally, Booth has developed an instructional literacy model that is a refinement of the instructional design principles placed within the library instructional context. She calls it the USER or Understand, Structure, Engage and Reflect model. Librarians should try and *understand* the instructional need or information gap of the user through analysis and identifying the problem, *structure* the instruction by establishing clear learning goals and objectives and involving learners in active learning, *engage* by implementing the instruction and ensuring participants are paying attention and involved and finally *reflect* on what went right and what could have been improved and refine accordingly.

Oakleaf and VanScoy (2010) have developed eight instructional strategies that can be used while providing reference services. These eight strategies are centered on three learning theories:

- *metacognition* (being intentional about one's thoughts or identifying what works best for them);
- *constructivism and active learning* (when people do, they learn; when they only listen or read, they forget);
- *social constructivism* (learning through social interaction with experts).

When working with users their *metacognition* can be used with four different instructional techniques – catch them being good (reinforce good information-seeking behavior and techniques), think aloud (verbalize how you would go about searching), show not tell (show them how to do it rather then tell them how to do it), and chunk it up (gather other potential problems and solutions they may need that are similar in nature to the question or problem they are presented with).

For *constructivist and active learning* there is only one strategy – let them drive. Once you have demonstrated, step aside and let them do it on their own. Successfully accomplishing the task will anchor their knowledge. Finally, the *social constructivist* approach incorporates two instructional strategies – be the welcome wagon (make the interaction extremely positive and welcoming), and make introductions, where you utilize the opportunity to help them as a way to show them other similarly related resources or ways of seeking information.

Regardless of the model used, instructional literacy will remain a cornerstone of librarianship well into the future. Library technology does simplify some things, but it makes others more complicated. The need for librarians to effectively assist information seekers will remain with us for many years to come.

Conclusion: user needs and library technology

Abstract: Where do humans fit in to the emerging world of information provision? Humans serve as the driving force behind what questions to ask and what answers to give, leveraging technology as a means to these ends. Technology is not a replacement for humans but rather an ally in carrying out repetitive tasks, thus enabling librarians to work interactively with users or spend more time ensuring their users' needs are met. It is not critical for your future survival to be the best at technology – just do not be at the end of the pack. Fear not technology but rather embrace the ways it can help you do the age-old job of meeting the information needs of users more efficiently.

Key words: systematic planning, humans, technology, library automation, mega, macro, micro.

Man is still the most extraordinary computer of all. (John F. Kennedy)

Whether the medium for transmitting information is a stone tablet, papyrus parchment, book page, computer screen, or a digital e-book, libraries around the world are still focused on meeting the information needs of their users. The technologies libraries use to achieve this objective, however powerful and innovative, remain a means to an end. Pablo Picasso once said: 'Computers are useless. They can only give you answers.' His point was that computers and technology in general can only do what we ask them or program them to do. In other words, technology without the human element is useless because it cannot provide answers to questions that remain unasked.

We must ask the relevant questions through systematic planning, budgeting and leveraging technology so that it most efficiently and effectively can facilitate seamless interactions between users and the information they seek. Robust networks with online access, functional computers and wireless connectivity are a given. Public libraries in particular have a mixed mission of continuing to provide access to technology that bridges the gap between society's haves and have-nots, while also being viewed as an extension of the online market place with the expectation that its services will be similar and up to par. Academic libraries are faced with a fluid environment. The changing nature of the college classroom and innovations in scholarly research require that librarians have a wide array of skills necessary to meet disparate user needs. School libraries will continue to increase their role in educational technology as a bastion of knowledge, instructional and technology support and professional development resources.

Within a systems framework, understanding the mega (societal), macro (organizational) and micro (operational) contexts in terms of concrete goals is paramount to knowing what to prioritize and how to plan for the future. Alignment of goals and resources is critical during the best of economic times. Constant and consistent evaluation in terms of the desired ends (outcomes) of your constituency, the available means (inputs) you are bringing to bear to meet the desired ends and the overall efficacy (quality) with which you are meeting the needs of your users is paramount to achieving success. This success will cost money and, as with any solid infrastructure and quality system, prevention over reaction through careful planning, cyclic maintenance and replacement and use of quality resources is key to ensuring your services are top rate, uninterrupted and seamlessly meeting the needs of your users.

Technology will continue to change at a rapid, dizzying pace. Rather than asking the question that begs to be asked in a defensive manner, 'How can we ever keep up?', we should reframe the question in an assertive, proactive fashion as, 'In what ways can we leverage technology to provide users with even greater access to our resources in a more efficient and effective manner?' You may be wondering how a library can ever keep up. A university colleague once shared a photo of a humorous picture depicting a lion chasing a zebra who was riding a motorcycle. The caption read something akin to: *Technology does it bigger, better and faster. You do not have to be the fastest member of your herd . . . just not the slowest.*

As a librarian or information professional the relationship between user services and technology resides squarely on your ability to ask the right questions, analyse the responses, set priorities and implement decisions to best meet the needs of your users. You do not have to be able to design or develop technology solutions, but you do need a broad understanding of current technologies and trends so you can serve as your organization's catalyst or advocate matching appropriate technological responses to specific user needs. In the world of library technology you do not have be at the bleeding edge in order to be successful; the pace of innovation should match your organization's strategic plan and your users' needs. But in order for your library to succeed in the twenty-first century, you will not want to be at the absolute end of the pack as an individual, department, or organization.

A recent visit by one of the authors to our downtown public library perfectly reflects the complex, sometimes uncomfortable, interactions between library staff, technology, user need and user satisfaction facing libraries today. It was after work, we were tired and the children had picked out their usual 20-plus books to check out for the week. We headed to the check-out area and there was a short line so we decided to use the self check-out stations for the first time. After taking a few moments to get acclimated with the technology, each of the children took turns scanning in their own books. The check-out machine voiced slow, repetitive commands each time we successfully scanned a book and the process continued until we were done. The librarians at the check-out desks always give us free bags to help us carry our books so my children approached a librarian and she gladly helped them, although she looked a little uncomfortable that we were using the self check-out stations instead of her (the transaction had taken much longer than it would have with a live librarian and the lines were long gone) so I asked her how she felt about them. She stated with a worried smile: 'I love them because it makes our lives easier but at the same time I fear that they will replace my job.' Despite her concern, however, she flashed us a beautiful, genuine smile as she wished us a great evening when we headed out the door.

As we were driving home a beautiful sunset was waning in the horizon, reflecting pink and gold shadows off the waters of one of North Carolina's numerous lakes, as I was pondering the librarian's words. The children were all eagerly devouring their new-found books, regular hard- and soft-cover books, in the back seat – exactly like we used to do when we were their age – despite having hundreds of e-books on iPad and Nook. They were oblivious to all the beauty around them because they were well immersed in the imaginative worlds spun by the books they were reading. The realization was crystal clear – the librarian did not have anything to worry about. The self check-out machine was slower, cold, yet efficient; it had its benefits where there was a line but we preferred the human contact and interaction of a librarian if possible and our children preferred the physical, tactile experience of reading hard- and soft-cover books.

The sun indeed is setting on yet another chapter of librarianship. As the light fades, the darkness of the unknown approaches, limiting how well and how far we can see into the distance. The sun, however, will arise again as users turn to library services in ever-increasing numbers and libraries continue to provide information access and services to the benefit of their users like they always have done. In the age of technology, where there are now in excess of 2 billion world-wide Internet users and information is free flowing across the globe, closer to home there is nearly 25 percent of the US population without access at all. In many ways, libraries are more critical than ever in ensuring equity and access to information and technology to all citizens; technology allows us to make these transactions more efficient and effective – but the bottom line is that Pablo Picasso had it right all along, as computers can only do what we want them to do. We must, however, ask the appropriate questions and do something with the answers, in a strategic and systematic fashion, as only humans can.

References

ACRL Research Planning and Review Committee (2010) *2010 Top Ten Trends in Academic Libraries: A review of the current literature*. Chicago, IL: ACRL.

ALA (American Library Association) (2000) *Statement on Library Use of Filtering Software*. Accessed 14 April 2011, from American Library Association: *http://www.ala.org/Template.cfm?Section=IF_Resolutions&Template=/ContentManagement/ContentDisplay.cfm&ContentID=13090*.

ALA (American Library Association) (2010) *The State of America's Libraries – 2010*. Chicago, IL: ALA.

Amazon (2009) *News Release*. Accessed 12 January 2011, from Amazon: *http://phx.corporate-ir.net/phoenix.zhtml?c=176060&p=irol-newsArticle&ID=1369429&highlight=*.

Association of American Publishers (2010) *Industry Statistics 2009*. Accessed 12 January 2011, from AAP: *http://www.publishers.org/main/IndustryStats/indStats_02.htm*.

Barrett, H. (2000) *The Portfolio Development Process*. Accessed 3 October 2010, from San Diego State College of Education: *http://edweb.sdsu.edu/courses/edtec700/ETP/addie.htm*.

Beaumont, C. (2009) *Half of World's Population Owns a Mobile Phone, UN Study Reveals*. Accessed 11 April 2011, from the *Telegraph*: *http://www.telegraph.co.uk/technology/news/4933263/Half-of-worlds-population-owns-a-mobile-phone-UN-study-reveals.html*.

Belkin, N., Oddy, R. and Brooks, H. (1982) 'ASK for information retrieval', *Journal of Documentation*, 38(2): 61–71.

Bertot, J. (2003) 'World Libraries on the Information Superhighway: Internet-based Services', *Library Trends*, Fall: 209–27.

Bertot, J. (2009) 'Public Access Technologies in Public Libraries' *Information Technologies in Libraries*, June.

Blanchard, K. and Bowles, S. (1993) *Raving Fans: A Revolutionary Approach to Customer Service*. New York: William Morrow and Company.

Bolt, N. and Stephan, S. (1998) *Strategic Planning for Multitype Library Cooperatives: A Planning Process*. Chicago, IL: American Library Association.

Booth, C. (2008) Developing Skype-based Reference Services. *Internet Reference Services Quarterly*, (13): 2–3.

Booth, C. (2010) *Build Your Own Instructional Literacy.* Accessed 17 April 2011, from *American Libraries: http://americanlibrariesmagazine.org/features/04302010/build-your-own-instructional-literacy.*

Bosman, J. (2010) *Times Will Rank E-Book Best Sellers.* Accessed 19 April 2011, from *The New York Times: http://www.nytimes.com/2010/11/11/books/11list.html?_r=1&ref=juliebosman.*

Breeding, M. (2011) 'The New Frontier', *Library Journal*, April: 24–34.

Buckingham, M. and Coffman, C. (1999) *First, Break All the Rules.* New York: Simon & Schuster.

Bucknall, T. (2010) Email Correspondence, 7 December, Greensboro, NC, USA.

Carolina Consortium (n.d.), *Carolina Consortium.* Accessed 19 April 2011, from *Carolina Consortium: http://library.uncg.edu/carolinaconsortium/available deals2011.asp.*

Case, D. (2007) *Looking for Information – A Survey of Research on Information Seeking, Needs and Behavior.* Oxford: Elsevier Ltd.

Chow, A. (2009) *UNCG Technology Boot Camp.* Accessed 19 August 2010, from UNCG LIS Department: *www.uncg.edu/lis.*

Chow, A. (2011) 'Information Architecture, Navigation and Usable Websites', Class Lecture, March. Greensboro, NC, USA.

Chow, A., Baity, C., Zamarripa, M., Chappell, P., Rachlin, D. and Vinson, C. (2011) 'Virtual Library Information Use and Users: A systems perspective'. Unpublished, Greensboro, NC, USA.

Chow, A., Bridges, M. and Commander, P. (2011) 'What does a typical library website look like? Results from a nationwide study.' A paper to be presented at the North Carolina Library Association, 4–7 October 2011, Hickory, NC, USA.

Chow, A., Chow, M. and Chow, E. (2011) 'Why Do You Like Virtual Worlds?' A. Chow, Interviewer, 18 April.

Chow, A. and Croxton, R. (2011) 'Academic libraries, information seeking behavior, and virtual reference services: Are there differences between university faculty, staff, and students?' A paper to be presented at the North Carolina Library Association, 4–7 October 2011, Hickory, NC, USA.

Chow, A., Smith, K. and Sun, K. (2010) 'Youth as Design Partners: Age-Appropriate Web Sites for Middle- and High-School Students'. Unpublished, Greensboro, NC, USA.

Clark, D. (2010) *ADDIE Timeline.* Accessed 1 October 2010, from Big Dog and Little Dog's Juxtaposition: *http://www.nwlink.com/~donclark/history_isd/addie.html.*

Clark, L. and Davis, D. (2009) *The State of Funding for Library Technology in Today's Economy.* Chicago, IL: American Library Association.

Clottes, J. (2003) *Return to Chauvet Cave, Excavating the Birthplace of Art: The First Full Report.* London: Thames & Hudson.

Comer, L.B. and Drollinger, T. (1999) 'Active Empathetic Listening and Selling Success: A Conceptual Framework', *Journal of Personal Selling & Sales Management*, Winter: 16–29.

CTIA (2010) *Wireless Quick Facts.* Accessed 11 April 2011, from The International Association for the Wireless Telecommunications Industry: *http://www.ctia.org/advocacy/research/index.cfm/aid/10323.*

Davis, C. (2011) A. Chow, Interviewer, 11 March.

Davis, D. (2009) *The Condition of U.S. Libraries: Academic Library Trends, 1999–2009.* Chicago, IL: American Library Association.

De Rosa, C., Cantrell, J., Cellentani, D., Hawk, J., Jenkins, L. and Wilson, A. (2005) *Perceptions of Libraries and Information Resources: A Report to the OCLC Membership.* Dublin: OCLC.

Dempsey, B. (2010) 'Do-It Yourself Libraries', *Library Journal*, July: 24–8.

DiMichele, P. (2007) Accessed 2 June, 2009, from University of Houston: *http://www.uh.edu/evolvinguh/documents/UH_usabilityMemo.pdf.*

Dougherty, W.C. (2009) 'Managing Technology During Times of Economic Downturns: Challenges and Opportunities', *The Journal of Academic Librarianship*, 35(4): 373–6.

Druin, A., Bederson, B., Boltman, A., Miura, A., Knotts-Callahan, D. and Platt, M. (1999) 'Children as our technology design partners', in A. Druin, *The Design of Children's Technology* (pp. 51–72). San Francisco, CA: Morgan Kaufmann.

Dugan, R.E. (2002) 'Information Technology Budgets and Costs: Do you know what your information technology costs each year?' *The Journal of Academic Librarianship*, 28(4): 238–43.

Ellis, K. (2011) A. Chow, Interviewer, 21 March.

Experian Hitwise (2011) *Top 20 Sites & Engines.* Accessed 14 April 2011, from Experian Hitwise: *http://www.hitwise.com/us/datacenter/main/dashboard-10133.html.*

Federal Trade Commission (2011) COPPA – Children's Online Privacy Protection Act. Accessed 2 June 2011, US Federal Trade Commission COPPA site: *http://www.coppa.org/coppa.htm.*

Fidel, R., Davies, R., Douglass, M., Holder, J., Hopkins, C., Kushner, E., et al. (1999) 'A Visit to the Information Mall: Web searching behavior of high school students', *Journal of the American Society of Information Science*, 50(1): 24–37.

Franklin, C. and Coustan, D. (2000) *How Operating Systems Work.* Accessed 13 April 2011, from *How Stuff Works: http://computer.howstuffworks.com/operating-system.htm.*

Freudenrich, C. and Carmack, C. (n.d.), *How Stuff Works.* Accessed 11 April 2011, from *How PDAs Work: http://electronics.howstuffworks.com/gadgets/travel/pda.htm.*

Frye, D. (2010) Google Document, 17 December. Reidsville, NC, USA.

Gabbott, M. and Hogg, G. (2001) 'The Role of Non-verbal Communication in Service Encounters: A conceptual framework', *Journal of Marketing Management*, 17: 5–26.

Griffey, J. (2010) 'Electronic Book Readers', in ALA, *Library Technology Reports* (pp. 7–19). Chicago, IL: ALA.

Harless, J. (1998) *The Eden Conspiracy: Educating for Accomplished Citizenship.* Wheaton, IL: Guild V Publications.

Hermann, J. (2008) *Red Box Rentals at Princeton Public Library.* Accessed 19 April 2011, from Tame the Web: *http://tametheweb.com/2009/07/01/red-box-rentals-at-princeton-public-library/.*

Hiller, S. and Self, J. (2004) 'From Measurement to Management: Using data wisely for planning and decision-making', *Library Trends*, 53(1): 129–55.

History of Operating Systems (n.d.), Accessed 13 April 2011, from Computer History: *http://www.computernostalgia.net/articles/HistoryofOperating Systems.htm.*

Horton, J. (2008) *How Wireless Internet Cards Work.* Accessed 19 April 2011, from *HowStuffWorks.com: http://communication.howstuffworks.com/ wireless-Internet-card.htm.*

Houghton-Jan, S. (2010) 'Internet Filtering', in ALA, *Library Technology Report* (pp. 25–33). Chicago, IL: ALA.

IEEE (2008) *Introduction to Ethernet.* Accessed 15 April 2011, from *Kioskia. net: http://en.kioskea.net/contents/technologies/ethernet.php3.*

IMLS (Institute of Museum and Library Service) (n.d.), *Frequently Asked Questions.* Accessed 16 April 2011, from *IMLS.gov: http://www.imls.gov/ applicants/faqs.shtm.*

IMLS (Institute of Museum and Library Service) (2006) *Status of Technology and Digitization in the Nation's Museums and Libraries.* Washington, DC: IMLS.

International Society for Performance Improvement (2011) *Human Performance Technology (HPT) Primer.* Accessed 2 June 2011, from ISPI: *http://www.afc-ispi.org/Repository/hptprimer.html.*

Internet World Stats (2010) *Internet Usage Statistics.* Accessed 14 April 2011, from Internet World Stats: *http://www.Internetworldstats.com/stats.htm.*

Jaegar, P. and Yan, Z. (2009) 'One Law with Two Outcomes: Comparing the implementation of CIPA in public libraries and schools', *Information Technology and Libraries*, March: 6–14.

Jones, T. (2001) *An Introduction to Digital Projects for Libraries, Museums and Archives.* Accessed 14 April 2011, from University Library, IL, at Urbana-Champaign: *http://images.library.uiuc.edu/resources/introduction.htm.*

Jordan, G.B. (2010) 'A theory-based logic model for innovation policy and evaluation', *Research Evaluation*, 263–73.

Jordan, P.W. (2001) *An Introduction to Usability.* Philadelphia, PA: Taylor & Francis.

Joseph, T. (2010) Email Correspondence, 21 December. Greensboro, NC, USA.

Kaufman, R. and Stakenas, R. (1981) *Needs Assessment and Holistic Planning.* Accessed 2 June 2011, from Association for Supervision and Curriculum Development: *http://www.ascd.org/ASCD/pdf/journals/ed_lead/el_198105_ kaufman.pdf.*

Kaufman, R., Watkins, R. and Guerra, I. (2001) 'The Future of Distance Learning: Defining and sustaining useful results', *Educational Technology*, 19–26.

Keller, J. (2000) Class Lecture. Tallahassee, FL, USA.

Kheterpal, S. (2003) *Pervasive Usability – Planning For an Uncertain Future.* Accessed 16 April 2011, from SitePoint: *http://blogs.sitepoint.com/planning-uncertain-future/.*

Kitsantas, A. and Chow, A. (2007) 'College Students Perceived Threat and Preference for Seeking Help in Traditional, Distributed and Distance Learning Environments', *Computers and Education*, 383–95.

Kochtanek, T. and Matthews, J. (2002) *Library Information Systems.* Westport, CT: Libraries Unlimited.

Krasner-Khait, B. (2001) *Survivor: The History of the Library*. Accessed 3 October 2010, from *History Magazine: http://www.history-magazine.com/libraries.html*.

Kroski, E. (2007) *Learning in a Virtual World*. Accessed 17 April 2011, from Womens Voices for Change: *http://womensvoicesforchange.org/learning-in-a-virtual-world.htm*.

Kyrillidou, M. (2002) 'From Input and Output Measures to Quality and Outcome Measures, or, from the User in the Life of the Library to the Library in the Life of the User', *The Journal of Academic Librarianship*, 28(1): 42–6.

KZero Worldswide (2011) *Virtual Worlds: 2011 and Beyond*. Cambridge, UK: KZero Worldswide.

Large, A., Beheshti, J., Nesset, V. and Bowler, L. (2006) 'Web portal design guidelines as identified by children through the processes of design and evaluation', *American Society for Information Science and Technology Proceedings*. Silver Springs, MD: American Society for Information Science and Technology.

Large, A., Behshti, J. and Rahman, T. (2002) 'Design for Criteria for Children's Web Portals: The users speak out', *Journal of the American Society for Information Science and Technology*, 53(2): 79–94.

Larson, L.C. (2010) 'Digital Readers: The next chapter', *The Reading Teacher*, 64(1): 15–22.

Lin, C. (2007) 'Organizational Website Design as a Rhetorical Situation', *IEEE Transactions on Professional Communication*, 50: 35–44.

Littman, J. and Connaway, L.S. (2004) 'A Circulation Analysis of Print Books and e-Books in an Academic Research Library', *Library Resources & Technical Services*, 48(4): 256–62.

May, P. (2009) *How to Avoid Spyware*. Accessed 13 April 2011, from *How Stuff Works: http://electronics.howstuffworks.com/how-to-tech/how-to-avoid-spyware.htm*.

McCrea, B. (2010) *5 K-12 Technology Trends for 2011*. Accessed 17 January 2011, from *THE Journal: http://the-journal.com/Articles/2010/12/02/5-K12-Technology-Trends-for-2011.aspx?Page=1*.

McDougall, P. (2010) *Tablets Will Replace One in Three PCs, Study Says*. Accessed 11 April 2011, from *Information Week: http://www.informationweek.com/news/storage/systems/showArticle.jhtml?articleID=228800307*.

McKendrick, J. (2011) *Funding and Priorities: The Library Resource Guide Benchmark Study on 2011 Spending Plans*. Medford, NJ: Information Today, Inc.

Merriam-Webster Online Dictionary (n.d.(a)), Accessed 2 June 2011, from *Merriam-Website Online Dictionary: http://www.merriam-webster.com/dictionary/goal*.

Merriam-Webster Online Dictionary (n.d.(b)), Accessed 2 June 2011, from *Merriam-Website Online Dictionary: http://www.merriam-webster.com/dictionary/computer*.

Merriam-Webster Online Dictionary (n.d.(c)), Accessed 13 April 2011, from *Merriam-Webster Online Dictionary: http://www.merriam-webster.com/dictionary/operating+system?show=0&t=1302708458*.

Merriam-Webster Online Dictionary (n.d.(d)), Accessed 13 April 2011, from Merriam-Website Online Dictionary: *http://www.merriam-webster.com/dictionary/malware.*

Merriam-Webster Online Dictionary (n.d.(e)), *Database.* Accessed 14 April 2011, from *Merriam-Webster Online Dictionary: http://www.merriam-webster.com/dictionary/database.*

Microsoft (2010) *Microsoft Office 2010 Engineering.* Accessed 4 November 2010, from Microsoft Office: *http://blogs.technet.com/b/office2010/archive/2010/01/22/office-2010-system-requirements.aspx.*

Morris, R.C. (1994) 'Toward a User Centered Information Service', *Journal of the American Society for Infomation Science,* 45(1): 20–30.

Morville, P. and Rosenfield, L. (2008) *Information Architecture for the World Wide Web.* Cambridge, MA: O'Reilly Media.

National Oceanic and Atmospheric Administration (NOAA) (2010) *Module 9: Making the Content Evaluation Process Continuous.* Accessed 3 October 2010, from National Oceanic and Atmospheric Administration: *http://webqa.csc.noaa.gov/wcde/images/Fig_06_010.gif.*

National Science Foundation (2009) *NSF Project Evaluation Guide* (2009) Washington, DC: The National Science Foundation.

Neerman, S. (2011) A. Chow, Interviewer, 30 March.

Nielsen, J. (2003) *Usability 101: Introduction to Usability.* Accessed 3 November 2010, from Jakob Nielsen's Alertbox: *http://www.useit.com/alertbox/20030825.html.*

Nielsen, J. (2005) *Usability of Websites for Teenagers.* Accessed 2 June 2009, from Jakob Nielsen's Alertbox: *http://www.useit.com/alertbox/teenagers.html.*

Nielsen, J. and Loranger, H. (2006) *Prioritizing Web Usability.* Berkeley, CA: New Riders.

Oakleaf, M. and VanScoy, A. (2010) 'Instructional Strategies for Digital Reference: Methods to facilitate student learning', *Reference & User Services Quarterly,* 49(4): 380–90.

Ott, J., Beard, M., Blue, D., Cleugh, C., Greenfield, D., Lee, T., et al. (2010) *Examining Internet Filtering Policies and Practices to Increase Student Technological Learning Opportunities.* Accessed 14 April 2011, from *Education News: http://www.educationnews.org/ed_reports/95634.html.*

PC.Com Encyclopedia. (n.d.), Accessed 13 April 2011, from *PC.Com Encyclopedia: http://www.pcmag.com/encyclopedia_term/0,2542,t=network+operating+system&i=47901,00.asp.*

Peters, T. (2008) 'Introduction', *Library Technology Reports,* 44(7): 5–6.

Pirolli, P. and Card, S. (1999) 'Information Foraging', *Psychological Review,* 106(4): 643–75.

Schifrin, M. (2007) *Rocking The Virtual World.* Accessed 17 April 2011, from Forbes.com: *http://www.forbes.com/forbes/2007/1224/103.html.*

Schlumpf, K. (2007) *Digitization: The Future is Now.* Accessed 14 April 2011, from North Surburban Library System: *http://www.nsls.info/articles/detail.aspx?articleID=124.*

SMART Goals (2010) *SMART Goal Setting.* Accessed 3 October 2010, from SMART Goals: *http://www.smart-goals.org/.*

Smith, A. (2010) *Pew Internet*. Accessed 19 April 2011, from Mobile Access 2010: *http://www.pewInternet.org/Reports/2010/Mobile-Access-2010.aspx.*

Sobel, D. (2003) *Internet Filters and Public Libraries*. Washington, DC: First Amendment Center.

Sperling, E. (2010) *Rise of the Tablet Computer*. Accessed 11 April 2011, from *Forbes Magazine: http://www.forbes.com/2010/09/10/ipad-apple-blackberry-technology-cio-network-tablets.html.*

Strickland, J. (2008) *Who owns the Internet?* Accessed 19 April 2011, from *HowStuffWorks.com: http://computer.howstuffworks.com/Internet/basics/who-owns-Internet.htm.*

Taylor, R. (1968) 'Question-negotiation and information seeking in libraries', *College and Research Libraries*, 28: 178–94.

Tyson, J. (2000) *How Firewalls Work*. Accessed 14 April 2011, from *How Stuff Works: http://computer.howstuffworks.com/firewall.htm.*

Tyson, J. (2001) *How LAN Switches Work*. Accessed 15 April 2011, from *How Stuff Works: http://computer.howstuffworks.com/lan-switch1.htm.*

US Department of Commerce National Telecommunications and Information Administration (2010) *Digital Nation 21st Century America's Progress Toward Universal Broadband Access*. Washington, DC: The US Department of Commerce National Telecommunications and Information Administration.

W.K. Kellogg Foundation (2004) *W.K. Kellogg Foundation Logic Model Development Guide*. Michigan, MI: W.K. Kellogg Foundation.

w3schools.com (n.d.(a)), *Browser Display Statistics*. Accessed 19 April 2011, from *w3schools.com: http://www.w3schools.com/browsers/browsers_display.asp.*

w3schools.com (n.d.(b)), *Browser Statistics*. Accessed 19 April 2011, from *w3schools.com: http://www.w3schools.com/browsers/browsers_stats.asp.*

w3schools.com (2011) *OS Platform Statistics*. Accessed 14 April 2011, from *w3cschools.com: http://www.w3schools.com/browsers/browsers_os.asp.*

Wagner, J.A. (2007) *Virtual World Population: 50 million by 2011*. Accessed 17 April 2011, from GIGAOM: *http://gigaom.com/2007/05/20/virtual-world-population-50-million-by-2011/.*

Wallace, D.P. and Naidoo, J. (2009) *Library and Information Science Education 2009 Statistical Report*. Chicago, IL: Association for Library and Information Science Education.

Watters, A. (2010) *Number of Virtual World Users Breaks 1 Billion, Roughly Half Under Age 15*. Accessed 17 April 2011, from ReadWriteWeb: *http://www.readwriteweb.com/archives/number_of_virtual_world_users_breaks_the_1_billion.php.*

Yuksel, A. (2008) 'Non-verbal Service Behavior and Customer's Affective Assessment', *Journal of Quality Assurance in Tourism*, 9(1): 57–77.

Index

23460619R00097

Made in the USA
Middletown, DE
25 August 2015